Biology of Ageing

TERTIARY LEVEL BIOLOGY

A series covering selected areas of biology at advanced undergraduate level. While designed specifically for course options at this level within Universities and Polytechnics, the series will be of great value to specialists and research workers in other fields who require a knowledge of the essentials of a subject.

Titles in the series:

Biological Membranes	Harrison and Lunt
Water and Plants	Meidner and Sheriff
Comparative Immunobiology	Manning and Turner
Methods in Experimental Biology	Ralph
Experimentation in Biology	Ridgman
Visceral Muscle	Huddart and Hunt
An Introduction to Biological Rhythms	Saunders
Biology of Nematodes	Croll and Matthews

Biology
of Ageing

Marion J. Lamb, B.Sc., Ph.D.

Lecturer in Zoology
Birkbeck College
London

Blackie

Glasgow and London

Blackie & Son Limited
Bishopbriggs
Glasgow G64 2NZ

450 Edgware Road
London W2 1EG

International Standard Book Number
Hardback 0 216 90327 0.

Printed in Great Britain by
Robert MacLehose and Company Limited
Printers to the University of Glasgow

Preface

THE AIM OF THIS BOOK IS TO BRING TOGETHER SOME OF THE MORE IMPORTANT
facts and ideas about the nature and causes of ageing processes. It is intended to provide students with an introduction to a subject of increasing interest
which has often been neglected in undergraduate biology courses.

It is not easy to give a balanced and objective account of our knowledge
of ageing. During the past decade, important and exciting advances have
been made in our understanding of ageing processes at the cellular and
molecular levels, and it is tempting to concentrate on the work in this area.
However, I believe that the observational and experimental work with whole
organisms is equally important. Some of the discoveries which were made
many years ago still have not been explained satisfactorily, and they should
not be forgotten. I have therefore tried to include in this book the most
significant results from the early studies of whole organisms, as well as those
from the more recent investigations at the cellular and molecular levels.

I have taken the approach of starting with whole organisms and populations of organisms, and gradually working down to the lower levels of
organization. Thus the book begins with chapters describing age-related
changes which can be seen in whole animals, and the way in which ageing
processes are reflected in the mortality statistics of populations. This is
followed by a discussion of longevity differences between and within species,
and an account of some of the ways in which life-span can be modified. The
next two chapters are devoted to a consideration of ageing of cells *in vivo*
and *in vitro*. In the final chapters, I have discussed some of the molecular
mechanisms which have been proposed to account for ageing changes, and
the way in which changes at the molecular level may be related to ageing of
whole organisms.

Since most of the early studies of ageing have been summarized in review
articles and books, I have in general referred the reader to these rather than
to the original sources. However, when describing work in areas where the
evidence is conflicting or controversial, or where no satisfactory review arti-

cle exists, I felt that it was necessary to cite original papers and to include references to these in the bibliography. I hope that the reference sections will enable the reader to trace, either directly or through a review article or a recent paper, all the investigations and theories discussed in the text.

Many people have helped me while I was preparing this book. I am grateful to them. In particular, I would like to thank the library staff at Birkbeck College for their help in tracing many of the references, Janet Chambers for her assistance in preparing the figures, Anne Kent for typing the manuscript, and Joan Round for reading a draft of the whole book and making so many helpful comments and criticisms.

MARION J. LAMB
Department of Zoology
Birkbeck College
London

Contents

CHAPTER ONE

INTRODUCTION

SOME MEN LIVE FOR MORE THAN 100 YEARS; NO MOUSE LIVES MORE THAN 4 years. Why is it that two mammalian species, so similar in many ways, should have such very different life-spans? A man of 75 usually has a more wrinkled skin, more grey hair, less muscular strength, poorer vision and hearing than he had when he was 25. He has become less fit and vigorous. What is the cause of the deteriorative changes which have occurred during this 50-year period? Can the changes be reversed? Could they have been prevented? Why is it that the chances of a 25-year-old man dying in the next year are less than one in a thousand, whereas the chances that a 75-year-old will die in the next year are almost one in ten? Is it possible to prolong the human life-span?

The aim of gerontology, the study of ageing and senescence, is to find the answers to questions like these. Senescence has been a subject of interest and speculation for centuries, and many causes and cures have been suggested for the deleterious changes which accompany increasing age. Speculations about the causes of senescence and differences in longevity have frequently been based on inadequate or incorrect factual information, and have led to hypotheses which cannot be tested. The suggested cures for senescence simply have not worked. However, during the past twenty years, gerontology has attracted the interest of an increasing number of biologists, and knowledge about many aspects of the subject is beginning to accumulate rapidly. Although we still know very little about the nature and causes of ageing changes and senescence, it certainly can no longer be said, as Medawar did in 1946, that

the problems of old age and natural death are hardly yet acknowledged to be within the province of genuine scientific enquiry.

In this chapter we shall consider the different approaches which are being used by gerontologists to investigate the nature and causes of ageing processes and senescence.

1.1 The definition of ageing and senescence

The terms *ageing* and *senescence* are familiar, but unfortunately they are rather imprecise. There is no general agreement among gerontologists about how they should be used. Usually *senescent* and *senescence* are used when talking about the changes which occur during the period of obvious functional decline in the later years of an animal's life-span. Some people use the term *ageing* for the same processes and period. Others use it in a much more general way, with *ageing* meaning simply growing older, and *ageing changes* being any changes related to age, regardless of when in the life-span they occur. Thus the onset of puberty might be described as an ageing change, but not as a senescence change. Although there may be advantages in using *ageing* in this general way, it is rather difficult to do so, because in common language *ageing* implies something more than simply getting older. For example, it would be unusual to talk of an ageing child. We would normally refer to a developing child, because in everyday English the word *ageing* carries with it the idea of decline and deterioration. Most biologists have tended to accept these connotations, and think of ageing as occurring only after maturity has been reached. In fact, as can be seen from some of the definitions given below, the terms *ageing* and *senescence* are frequently used interchangeably.

There have been many formal definitions of ageing processes and senescence. Medawar (1952) suggested that senescence could be defined as

that change of the bodily faculties and sensibilities and energies which accompanies ageing, and which renders the individual progressively more likely to die from accidental causes of random incidence. Strictly speaking, the word "accidental" is redundant, for all deaths are in some degree accidental. No death is wholly "natural"; no one dies *merely* of the burden of the years.

Strehler (1962) defined senescence as

the changes which occur generally in the post-reproductive period and which result in a decreased survival capacity on the part of the individual organism.

Ageing processes have been defined by Maynard Smith (1962) as

those which render individuals more susceptible as they grow older to the various factors, intrinsic or extrinsic, which may cause death

and Comfort (1960) said that ageing is

an increased liability to die, or an increasing loss of vigour, with increasing chronological age, or with the passage of the life cycle.

It is worth while emphasizing and amplifying some of the points which are made or implied in these definitions. Firstly, the changes which occur during ageing are deleterious; they increase the chances that an animal will die. Ageing therefore involves a decrease in the ability of an animal to cope with its environment. Secondly, the deleterious age-related changes are cumulative. Death, the ultimate result of ageing, is sudden, but the process of ageing involves a progressive increase in the probability of dying. A third characteristic of ageing and senescence, which is implicit in most of the definitions which have been given, is that the processes involved are common to all members of a species and are inescapable consequences of getting older. That is to say, ageing and senescence are fundamental intrinsic properties of living organisms.

1.2 Ageing and the length of life

Sometimes it is helpful to visualize the characteristics of ageing and the relation between ageing processes and the length of life in the way illustrated in figure 1.1. On the left of the diagram the ageing of an individual has been shown as a loss of *vitality* with time. *Vitality* is a term which has been used by a number of gerontologists, including Raymond Pearl, one of the founders of modern experimental gerontology. By *vitality* we mean nothing more than the ability to sustain life, the ability to survive. This gets less as age increases. Quite deliberately no scale has been put on either of the axes in figure 1.1. If the time scale was linear, it would imply that ageing is a linear function of time; there is no reason to think that this is true. By omitting a scale we are leaving open the question of whether the rate of ageing increases, decreases, remains constant or fluctuates in any particular time interval. The straight line parallel to the time axis is a death threshold: when vitality falls below this threshold, death occurs. The level of the death threshold reflects the severity of the conditions to which the individual is exposed. If conditions are severe, the threshold will be higher, and hence the length of life will be shorter.

The right-hand section of figure 1.1 is an attempt to make the picture of ageing and longevity a little more realistic. Ageing and times of death for four individuals are shown. The first point to note is that the individuals start life with different amounts of vitality. Secondly, the rate of loss of vitality, or rate of ageing, is not the same for all individuals. The justification for these two features will be discussed in later chapters. For our present purpose it is sufficient to say that there is evidence that longevity is influenced by an animal's genotype and, since there are usually genetic differences between individuals in a population, either the rate of ageing or the initial level of vitality or both of these characters may be different in different individuals.

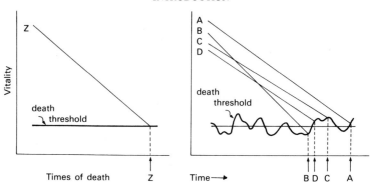

Figure 1.1   Diagrammatic representations of ageing (see text for explanation).

The representation of the death threshold has also been modified in the right-hand part of the figure. The environmental challenges that an animal has to cope with are never completely constant, so the death threshold has been shown as fluctuating around a mean value.

Simple two-dimensional illustrations such as those provided in figure 1.1 may sometimes be misleading when they are used to visualize a little-understood but undoubtedly complex process such as ageing. It is not difficult to criticize some of the features of the diagram. For example, even in the right-hand part of the figure it has been assumed that there is no relation between the rate of ageing and the death threshold. This is not necessarily true. Suppose that the cause of the increase in the death threshold is a disease epidemic or a very cold spell. Is it correct to assume, as is implied in the diagram, that the rate of ageing is unaffected by these factors? There is no justification for this assumption, because we do not know the extent to which the rate of ageing depends on environmental stresses. Similarly, the diagram shows only one death threshold and therefore suggests that the factors which may cause death are, at any instant, identical for all individuals. This is most unrealistic. In spite of these and other defects, the illustration is of value because it does make it easier to see how complex the relation between ageing processes and the time of death is likely to be. Individual A ages more rapidly than individual C, yet it has a longer life-span than C. Individual D lives longer than B, yet if these individuals had been challenged by a very severe stress at the beginning of their lives, B, the individual with the shorter life-span, would have had a greater chance of surviving than D. The point to note is that the length of life does not depend simply on the rate at which ageing processes are occurring.

1.3 The measurement of ageing changes

According to the definitions given earlier, ageing changes show themselves in two ways. Firstly, they result in an increase with time in the chances of dying; secondly, ageing involves a decline in the ability of an individual to withstand the factors which are likely to cause death – a loss of vigour. Either times of death or age-related decrease in functional properties may be used to demonstrate that ageing changes are occurring. To some extent, they can also be used to measure the rate at which ageing is occurring.

Since death is a single event in an individual's life-span, the time at which it happens can tell us nothing about the ageing of that individual. However, if a population of similar individuals is studied, then the distribution of the times of death should tell us whether or not ageing processes are occurring. If ageing changes are not taking place, then the chances that an animal will die in any particular interval of time, such as a day or a year, will not be related to the age of the animal; if they are occurring, the chances that death will occur in the particular interval will increase with increasing age of the animal. The way in which mortality distributions in populations can be used in studies of ageing is discussed in chapter 3. For the present, it is, however, worth stating again that the longevity of an individual and the average life-span of a population are determined not only by the rate of ageing, but also by the size and nature of the environmental stresses to which the individuals are subjected.

In many ways, if we wish to understand the nature of ageing processes and to measure the rate at which they are taking place, studying the age-dependent changes that occur within an individual's life-span should be more profitable than studying the actual time of death. What we want to know is what *vitality* is, what causes it to decline, and what determines the rate at which it declines. However, until we know the answers to these questions, it is very difficult to decide what aspects of the physiology or biochemistry of an individual are going to be adequate measurements of ageing. Many age-related changes in various physiological and biochemical functions have been found, but determining which of these are important and how they are inter-related is not easy.

One of the problems encountered in any study of the mechanisms underlying ageing is deciding when in the life-span the study should begin. Although the terms *ageing* and *senescence* are usually associated with the deleterious changes occurring in the latter part of life, it would be foolish to limit a study of ageing to just that period. The obvious effects of ageing processes may not be seen until late in life, but the processes themselves may start much earlier. In spite of the fact that it is convenient to divide the life-span of mammals into stages such as the prenatal period, neonatal period, infancy, childhood, adolescence, maturity and senescence, these are not really distinct unrelated periods. Even in holometabolous insects which have well-defined egg, larval, pupal and imaginal stages, many of the tissues are formed very early in development and remain apparently unchanged throughout the later stages. Therefore not only is it difficult to separate developmental and ageing processes, it is also probably undesirable to do so. We must remember that although it may be necessary or convenient to begin studies of ageing changes at a particular time, such as birth or maturity in a mammal or imaginal emergence in an insect, changes which do not manifest themselves until late in life may well have been initiated long before they become apparent.

1.4   Levels of organization at which ageing can be studied

We have discussed how the definitions of ageing and senescence point to two ways in which ageing processes can be shown to occur: it is possible to study ageing either by investigating the times of death within a population of similar individuals, or by following a time-dependent decline in the physiological performance of individual animals. Quite clearly, though, in order to understand ageing it is necessary to study the phenomenon at levels of organization lower than that of the whole animal. It is known that some organs, tissues, cells, cell organelles and molecules change – and frequently deteriorate – with time.

It is a characteristic of living organisms that when parts are damaged or worn out they can often be repaired or replaced. For example, as the cells on the surface of the skin of mammals are sloughed off, they are replaced by cells from lower layers which, in turn, are ultimately derived from relatively undifferentiated basal cells capable of repeated mitotic division. Similarly, mammalian red blood cells are constantly being destroyed and replaced by new cells. Many enzyme molecules are known to turn over very rapidly, and even for molecules such as DNA which do not turn over, it is known that enzymes exist which are capable of repairing some types of damage to the molecule. Yet in spite of this widespread capacity for repair and replacement, deteriorative changes can be seen in the cells and tissues as the organism gets older. What is the relation between these deteriorative changes and the ageing of the whole animal? What is the relationship between the longevity and ageing of cells, organelles and molecules, and the longevity and senescence of the whole animal? If the causes of ageing and senescence in a particular short-lived cell type, such as an intestinal cell, are understood, will this knowledge be sufficient to provide a model for ageing in the whole animal?

These questions are not easy to answer. They will be considered in more detail in later chapters, but at this stage it is necessary to emphasize three points. Firstly, the fact that molecules, organelles and cells turn over, that they "die" and are degraded and replaced by new ones, does not necessarily mean that they are showing ageing and senescence. According to our definitions, ageing processes are occurring only if the molecules, organelles and cells become more likely to be degraded as they become older. This would be so if they showed an age-related deterioration that made them capable of being recognized as less efficient by the systems responsible for their destruction. On the other hand, if the degradation of cells or subcellular elements is a method of regulating their number or concentration, then their destruction might be an entirely random process quite unrelated to their age. Although studying the length of life of subcellular elements and molecules is difficult, present knowledge suggests that many enzyme molecules are destroyed at times unrelated to their age, and therefore that they do not show evidence of ageing in the sense that we are using the word.

The second point that has to be considered is what constitutes the length of life of cells. Many cells end their "life-span" not by death and degradation, but by division. Are these cells to be considered immortal, or do they show ageing changes? Recently there has been considerable interest in the senescence of these cells and in their possible significance for understanding the senescence of the whole animal. For cells which are capable of division, interest centres not so much on the life-span and ageing of the individual cells, but on the cell lineage. In other words, what is studied is *clonal* ageing, the longevity and senescence of the whole line of cells arising from repeated mitotic divisions, rather than ageing of single cells. For some Protozoa it is also more usual to think of ageing and senescence as characteristics of clones rather than of individuals.

The final point to emphasize while considering the levels at which ageing processes may be studied is one which will be referred to repeatedly in later chapters, namely that it is very difficult to isolate the effects of the ageing of the parts of an animal from the ageing of the whole animal itself. If, as the animal ages, a change is observed in a particular type of cell or tissue, is it occurring because the cell or tissue itself is undergoing intrinsic ageing processes independent of those occurring elsewhere in the body, or is the change simply a secondary consequence of the deterioration of some other part of the animal? Some of the ways in which people have attempted to find a solution to this problem will be discussed in chapters 6 and 7. It is a difficult problem to solve, but a very important one.

Although there are many technical and interpretative difficulties involved in studies of senescence at the tissue, cellular and subcellular levels, these studies are essential, since the senescence of the whole animal must ultimately be caused by changes occurring at these lower levels of organization. When cells and molecules are capable of extensive replacement, we have to know whether or not the new cells and molecules formed are the same as those which they replace. When cells and molecules are not replaced during the course of an animal's life-span, we need to know the extent to which they are damaged and can be repaired. Only by studying ageing at the lower levels of organization will we understand the nature and causes of the age-related decline in the functional performance of the whole animal.

1.5   The choice of organism for ageing research

Since most, if not all, living organisms show an age-related decline in functional capacity, ageing can be studied in a wide variety of animals and plants. Most studies have been made with the relatively short-lived mammals, particularly rats and mice, and it is assumed that the causes and manifestations of ageing in these animals are likely to be similar to those in man. However, ageing changes and senescence have also been investigated in animals such as fish, insects, nematodes and even unicellular organisms. These differ from each other and from mammals in a large number of ways. Is there any reason to think that the causes and nature of ageing processes are the same in all these organisms? Can we extrapolate from one organism to another?

At present there is no reason to assume that the processes of ageing are the same in all organisms, and we have to accept the possibility that there may be differences in the causes as well as the manifestations of ageing in different organisms. Nevertheless, many of the hypotheses which have been developed to explain senescence have assumed that the basic mechanisms involved will be found to be the same in all organisms. If this assumption proves to be correct, then studies of ageing in lower animals may provide very valuable information rather more easily than those with mammals. Not only do many invertebrate animals have shorter life-spans than mammals, most also have the advantage of being very much cheaper to rear and maintain in large numbers. Apart from the economic considerations, some non-mammalian organisms have characteristics which make them very suitable for studying some aspects of ageing. For example, if one is interested in seeing how changes in metabolic rate affect ageing changes, it is easier to use a poikilotherm than a homeotherm; if one is interested in the changes which occur in non-dividing cells, it is easier to study them in a nematode or an adult insect, where cell division is rare, than in a vertebrate, in which most cells are capable of dividing. If the ultimate aim of gerontology is to understand the nature and causes of ageing processes and senescence in man, then although studies with non-mammalian organisms can never be a substitute for studies of man and other mammals, they can at least be used to test the many hypotheses which suggest that there is a single cause of ageing for all animals.

CHAPTER TWO

MANIFESTATIONS OF AGEING IN INDIVIDUALS

AS MEN GET OLDER, THERE ARE NOTICEABLE CHANGES IN THEIR APPEARANCE
and also in their general physical capabilities. Often it is possible to judge a
person's age fairly accurately from his general appearance, but it is also true
that appearances can sometimes be very misleading. We all know that the
age at which hair begins to grey, or the skin begins to wrinkle, varies considerably between individuals. Furthermore, sometimes the different indicators of age are not consistent: a person may seem to be "old" because
he has grey hair, yet his hearing and vision may be as good as those of a
young man; conversely, a man who is physically decrepit may have no grey
hair at all. In order to study rates of ageing, we have to decide which
features are likely to give the best indication of what is often called
biological age or *physiological age*, rather than *chronological age*. In other
words, we need to know which of the obvious manifestations of age provide
the best way of measuring the "loss of vitality" and predicting potential
longevity. In this chapter we shall consider some of the age-related changes

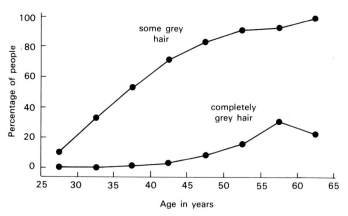

Figure 2.1 Rate of hair greying for 3872 Australian men and women with medium colour
hair (based on data of Keogh and Walsh, 1965).

which occur in man and other animals, and the ways in which they are measured. It will be clear that assessing the rate at which ageing processes are occurring is not at all easy.

2.1 Ageing changes in man

One of the most obvious signs of human ageing is the greying of hair. As figure 2.1 shows, with increasing age more and more people have some grey hair. This figure is based on data obtained from a survey of Australian men and women, in which hair-greying was assessed in three categories: *complete greying*, *any greying*, and *no greying*. Although there were problems in distinguishing grey hair in fair-haired people, when allowance was made for this, there was no evidence of any differences in the rate of greying among people of different hair colours, or between men and women. It should be noted that greying begins before the age of 30 and steadily increases.

Figure 2.2 shows the way in which skin elasticity changes with age. This measurable change in skin properties is probably associated with one of the obvious visible signs of ageing, namely changes in skin texture and appearance. The figure shows that in both sexes there is a gradual rise in the modulus of elasticity, but that this "stiffening up" is more marked in women

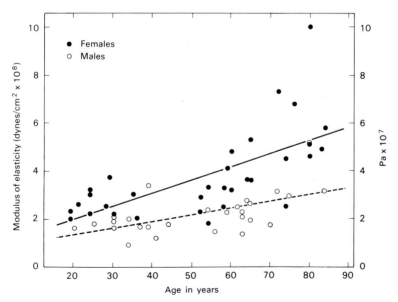

Figure 2.2 Age-related changes in the *in vivo* elasticity of human fore-arm skin (based on data of Grahame and Holt, 1969).

than in men, in spite of the fact that women have the longer life-span. As we shall discuss in chapter 6, the age-related change in skin elasticity is probably caused in part by changes in the collagen molecules which form a high proportion of the protein in skin.

Apart from visible changes in appearance, one of the most familiar signs of ageing is a general loss of strength. Several different methods have been used to measure this change. Figure 2.3 shows the results from measuring hand-grip strength. The values plotted are the averages for each decade of life, and they show that after an initial rise there is a decline in grip strength for both men and women. These data come from a preliminary study of a number of physiological functions in over 400 people in Hiroshima. The aim of the study is to measure a number of variables which are known to change with age, and from these to attempt to determine "biological age" and ultimately to relate this to mortality in the subjects surveyed. Figure 2.4 shows the results from two other series of tests made in this survey; both blood pressure and the vital capacity of the lungs show marked changes after the age of 40. Hearing, visual acuity, vibration perception, manual dexterity and mental reaction time were also tested, and all showed deteriorations, particularly beyond the age of forty.

Some of the most striking age-related changes are revealed by studying the responses of the body to a physiological challenge. The pH, ion concentration, temperature, levels of metabolites and of food substances in the internal environment of mammals are normally maintained within very narrow limits. Numerous feedback mechanisms tend to restore the composition

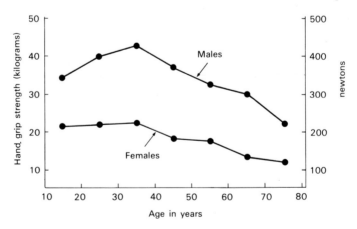

Figure 2.3   Changes in hand grip strength with age (based on data of Hollingsworth *et al.*, 1965).

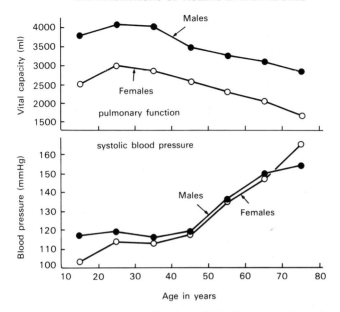

Figure 2.4 Changes in pulmonary function and blood pressure with age (based on data of Hollingsworth *et al.*, 1965).

of the internal environment to normal if a natural or artificially applied stress causes it to change. It is clear, however, that these homeostatic control mechanisms become less efficient as age increases. For example, normally the glucose level in blood shows very little change with age, but if glucose is injected into the blood, the rate of restoration to the normal level shows a marked dependence on age: it is far slower in old people than in young. This decline in the efficiency and effectiveness of the homeostatic regulatory mechanisms could be due to deficiencies in one or all of a number of interdependent tissues and cells. In the case of glucose, the muscles and liver are important for its storage, the pancreas is involved in the production of insulin, which regulates storage and mobilization, and the kidneys are involved in getting rid of excess amounts.

Nathan Shock has made extensive studies of ageing changes in man and other mammals, and has concluded that the functions which show the greatest change are those which involve the co-ordinated activity of a number of organ systems. Those which show little or no change usually involve only a single organ or system. For example, nerve conduction velocity changes by only about 10% between the ages of 20 and 90, whereas the maximum breathing capacity decreases by 50%. The former is a measurement of the performance of nerves only, the latter depends on the efficiency and co-ordination of both the nervous and muscular systems. Shock (1974) has suggested that from a physiological point of view, ageing involves primarily an impairment or breakdown of control mechanisms. The more complex a task is in biological terms, the more likely it is to show an age-related deterioration.

It is impossible to consider all the age-related changes in physiological functions that are known to occur in man. Others will be referred to in later chapters. For the moment it is sufficient to say that almost every system which has been studied shows some change. There is no difficulty in finding measurable age-related changes. The problem is deciding what these changes mean in relation to "biological age" and the probability of dying. One of the best indicators of age is hair-greying; yet it is difficult to believe that this has much to do with the increased likelihood of dying as age increases. Skin elasticity is a good indicator of age; yet, according to the results shown in figure 2.2, if judged only by skin elasticity, a woman of 30 has the same biological age as a man of 80. In the study of Japanese subjects, many of the tests gave results which showed that the main changes occurred in the latter half of life, but hair-greying and skin elasticity changes certainly begin long before this. Which of the age-dependent changes is going to provide the most useful measurement of the rate of ageing? At present it seems unlikely that any one measurement will ever be sufficient. A "test-battery", as Alex Comfort calls it, is needed. Comfort (1969) has suggested that it is now possible and desirable to organize a battery of tests to measure the rate of ageing in normal human subjects. He argues that if enough suitable characteristics are measured, then it should be possible to estimate biological age and the rate at which ageing changes are progressing. It is important that we should be able to assess biological age. Our understanding of ageing may soon progress to the point where it is possible to suggest which factors do or could influence the rate of ageing in man. Unless we have some measurement of ageing other than mortality rates, it is going to take an unrealistically long time to see whether a drug (or environmental or nutritional factor) is capable of affecting the rate of ageing processes.

2.2   Measuring rates of ageing in human populations

One of the difficulties in attempting to construct a battery of tests for measuring the rate of ageing in humans is that most of the data we have at present come from *cross-sectional* or *point-of-time* studies. In cross-sectional studies, measurements of the characteristic under investigation are made in samples of people of different ages. The information obtained from these studies is undoubtedly valuable, but it may sometimes be misleading if it is assumed that the way in which the *average* value changes from one age group to the next represents the change which occurs in an *individual* with the passage of time. A possible consequence of making this assumption is shown in figure 2.5, which illustrates the way in which some hypothetical factor might be related to age for five individuals. It is assumed that performance reaches a maximum somewhere between 15 and 30 years of age, and then falls. The rate at which the rise and fall happens is slower in some individuals than in others. The effect of taking the average value for the five individuals is to suggest that physiological performance changes very little between 15 and 30 years of age, whereas in fact for each individual the changes occurring during this period are as great as those in any other period. By taking the average value, the picture is blurred. In order to obtain a true picture of the rate at which ageing changes are occurring, it is really necessary to make *longitudinal* studies – that is to say, to follow the changes which occur in individuals over a period of years. To do this for man is rather difficult, and obviously takes a long time. Ideally longitudinal studies should be made on normal healthy people rather than those in hospitals and other institutions; yet it is only in institutions that people are likely to be available for long-term study. It is difficult to keep track of nor-

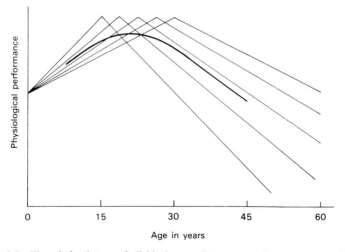

Figure 2.5   The relation between individual rates of change and the average rate of change. Thin lines represent individuals, the thick line is the average value.

mal healthy subjects over a period of years, and so far very few adequate long-term longitudinal studies of ageing changes have been made.

A further difficulty in the interpretation of studies of the rates of ageing based on cross-sectional data is that inevitably samples of old people are much more highly selected than those of young people. People who die young cannot be included in a sample of old people! Since this is so, if the age-related character being measured is one whose deterioration contributes to the increased probability of dying, then the samples of old people are likely to be made up of individuals in whom this character has changed least. Consequently, cross-sectional studies may well underestimate the extent of age-dependent changes.

Perhaps the most important of the many problems associated with interpreting data from man is that of knowing how to allow for the fact that the environmental factors to which various age groups have been exposed are likely to have been very different. If we think of a sample of 70-year-olds and a sample of 20-year-olds alive at the present time, then we have to remember that in their childhood and youth the 20-year-olds will have had the benefits of 50 years of advances in medicine and public health which the 70-year-olds did not have when they were young. How can we tell whether differences between 20-year-olds and 70-year-olds are due to ageing *per se*, or whether they are due to the undoubtedly harsher conditions to which the 70-year-olds were subjected during childhood and adolescence? For man it is almost impossible to know which changes are due to different environmental conditions and which are due to increased age.

2.3   Ageing changes in laboratory animals

Rather less is known about the physiology and pathology of most laboratory animals than is known about the physiology and pathology of man. Nevertheless, they have many advantages for physiological studies of ageing, because most of the problems associated with sampling from human populations need not occur with experimental animals. It should be possible to make longitudinal studies since the life-spans of most of the common laboratory animals are short. Even if cross-sectional studies are made, the data are usually easier to interpret. There are two reasons for this. First of all, it is possible to control the environment in which the animals are maintained. Thus the problem of different age groups having been subjected to different conditions can be avoided. Secondly, the effects of heterogeneity in the rates of ageing, such as is shown in figure 2.5, can be minimized by using animals which are genetically uniform and are therefore likely to have similar rates of ageing. However, the main reason why animal studies can contribute so much to the understanding of the physiological decline which accompanies increasing age is that it is possible to subject animals to controlled stresses, and to test their capacity to respond to those stresses. Sometimes the test made is simply the ability to survive a specific stress, but attempts have also been made to evaluate the efficiency of homeostatic mechanisms by measuring the rate at which particular functions return to their normal level after a stress has been applied.

The results of two studies of the responses of animals to a potentially lethal stress are shown in figure 2.6. The animals used were the fruit fly *Drosophila melanogaster* and the mouse; the stress was exposure to a single acute dose of ionizing radiation. As we shall discuss in chapter 5, ionizing radiation does have long-term effects on longevity, but here we are not concerned with these. What is shown in the figure is the immediate effect of radiation, as measured by the LD_{50}. The LD_{50} is the dose which will kill 50% of the animals within a short period after exposure. For the mouse the period used is 30 days ($LD_{50\,(30)}$); for *Drosophila* it is a day ($LD_{50\,(1)}$). Mice which die during the 30-day period usually show signs of severe damage to the gastrointestinal tract and haematopoietic system, and death is frequently due to haemorrhage or secondary infections. For *Drosophila* the causes of death are not known, although it has been suggested that damage to the nervous system may be involved. Like many insects, adult flies are very resis-

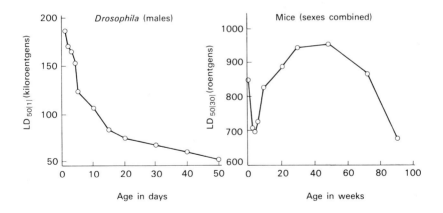

Figure 2.6   Age-related changes in the LD_{50} for ionizing radiation for *Drosophila* (based on data of Baxter and Blair, 1967) and the mouse (based on data of Crosfill *et al.*, 1959).

tant to the harmful effects of radiation, so the LD_{50} is usually expressed in kiloroentgens or kilorads, rather than in roentgens or rads. Both the mouse and *Drosophila* show a clear increase in sensitivity to ionizing radiation between maturity and old age. The data for mice show that they are also very sensitive around the weaning period at about 4 weeks, and that maximum resistance occurs at 30-50 weeks of age. Adult *Drosophila* show a steady loss of resistance with age, but it is known that the larval and pupal stages are much more sensitive than the adult. Therefore, although the dose-response curves for the two species are different both quantitatively and qualitatively, they do show that the ability to recover from the immediate effects of ionizing radiation decreases with advancing age.

There are many other studies which show that old animals succumb to stresses more quickly than young animals. For example, the volume of blood which rats can lose before death decreases with increasing age; the ability of mice to survive at very low temperatures decreases with increasing age. *Drosophila* becomes more sensitive to the lethal effects of high non-physiological temperatures and to desiccation with increasing age; an age-related increase in sensitivity to toxic substances has been found in a number of different species. There are far fewer studies of the ability to adapt to stress, or the rate of recovery from a stress. It has been shown that following immersion in ice-cold water for 3 minutes, adult rats recover normal body temperature in an average of 65.0 ± 2.2 min, whereas middle-aged rats take 90.0 ± 5.7 min, and old rats take 110.0 ± 6.9 min. The increased recovery time is due to changes in both the size of the initial drop in body temperature and the rate of recovery.

Figure 2.7 shows the results of another investigation of the ability of rats to adapt to an environmental stress. The stress was a reduction of the barometric pressure to 350 mmHg. This pressure is that which would be found at an altitude of 6500 metres. Within a few hours of reducing the pressure, the rectal temperature of the rats fell by several degrees, but there were no age-related differences in the size of this initial drop. However, differences were seen in the subsequent temperature changes. Young rats kept in the low-pressure atmosphere could adapt to the conditions, and their body temperature was restored to a normal level within 4-5 days. In contrast to this, rats more than one year old were unable to restore body temperature to normal values even after 10 days. The cause of the failure of middle-aged and old rats to adapt to the reduced pressure is not known, but clearly the homeostatic control mechanisms were less efficient in the older animals.

Some people have suggested that another indirect method can be used to

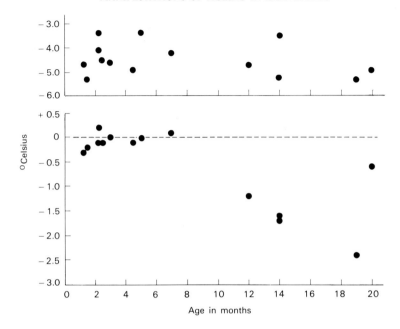

Figure 2.7 Changes in the rectal temperature of rats kept in a low-pressure atmosphere. The upper graph shows the maximum fall in rectal temperature; the lower graph shows the difference between the normal rectal temperature at the beginning of the experiment and the temperature after 4–5 days "adaptation" to the low-pressure atmosphere (based on data of Flückiger and Verzár, 1955).

assess changes in the efficiency of homeostatic mechanisms. This method involves measuring the size of the differences in some property between genetically similar individuals of the same age. The measurement used is the *variance*, a measurement of the amount of spread of the readings around the average value. It is argued that even if there is no change in the *average* performance of some function, if the variance increases with age it is evidence of a deterioration in that function. Increasing variance reflects declining adequacy of homeostasis. The reasoning behind this argument is as follows. An efficient homeostatic mechanism will, if a disturbance takes a particular system away from its optimum level of activity, restore the normal level quickly before the deviation has become large. Consequently, in an examination of a number of very similar animals kept in the same environment, the measurements will all be close to the normal optimum value if homeostasis is efficient. Conversely, with an inefficient homeostatic mechanism, the size of the fluctuations around the optimum level will be larger, and the speed with which the normal level is restored will be slower. Thus, even if the average value of a physiological function remains the same, the variance will be greater, because in some individuals the level will be a long way from the normal value. Figure 2.8 shows the way in which the variances of body weight, osmotic fragility of the erythrocytes, haematocrit, and the ability to survive the toxic effects of sodium pentobarbital increase with age in an inbred strain of mice. The variance found in the youngest age group was given the value 1, and the variances found at greater ages have been expressed as multiples of this. Thus the variance of body weights of 16-month-old mice was four times as great as that of four-month-old mice. The mean value for each of the four characters studied showed only slight changes with age but, as the figure shows, for all four of them the variance increased. There is evidence from other studies that short-lived strains of mice show a more rapid increase in variance than long-lived strains. This is what would be expected if variance estimates the homeostatic capacity and if the ability to maintain homeostasis is important for the maintenance of life.

2.4　Ageing, injury and disease

One of the signs of ageing which is all too familiar to many of us is the increasing incidence of many different types of disease. As we get older, we frequently begin to show symptoms of arthritis, osteoporosis,

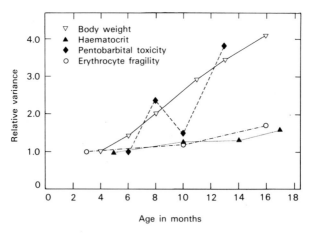

Figure 2.8　Age-related changes in the variance of body weight, erythrocyte fragility, pentobarbital toxicity, and haematocrit for male mice (redrawn from Storer, 1965).

atherosclerosis, or malignant tumours, for example. When old people die, it is often very difficult to pinpoint the exact cause of death, because pathological changes can be seen in so many tissues and organs. In developed countries, the major causes of death are at present cardiovascular diseases and cancer, but it has been calculated that if it was possible to eliminate both of these, average life-span would be increased by only 6 or 7 years. If we did not die of cancer or cardiovascular disease, we would soon die of something else.

Most of the diseases which we associate with old age may well be initiated long before they become clinically obvious. For example, the early signs of changes in the arteries which are thought to precede atherosclerosis – a condition which may ultimately cause death by a stroke or heart attack – can often be detected *post mortem* before the age of 20. With increasing age, the number and size of the lesions in the arteries increase, and their structure changes. The problem is, are diseases like this the causes or the consequences of ageing processes? Are they innate and inevitable, or are they caused by environmental factors?

From time to time it has been suggested that age-dependent loss of vigour is simply the result of pathological changes initiated by earlier disease or by other forms of wear and tear and injury to the body. In the early part of this century, Metchnikoff, the discoverer of phagocytosis, proposed that many of the adverse effects of increasing age would be prevented if harmful microbes could be eliminated from the body. In particular, he believed that the bacteria in the large intestine were harmful because they produced toxins which passed into the lymph and blood, and led to degeneration of other parts of the body. He suggested that elimination of the harmful gut bacteria, elimination of syphilis, and suppression of alcoholism would prevent many of the pathological symptoms of old age and probably increase the length of life.

Although in this extreme form the idea that ageing is due to disease now receives little support, it cannot be denied that previous disease and injury must make some contribution to the age-related increase in the probability of dying. Animals are constantly exposed to infections which are likely to cause minor damage to cells and tissues. In mammals, teeth are damaged and lost, and cannot be replaced. Injuries such as limb fractures occur; usually they heal, but the healed limb may not be as efficient as it was before the fracture occurred. Thus, as an animal gets older it will – simply because it has lived longer – accumulate more and more of the type of damage associated with minor diseases and injuries.

At present, few people seem prepared to accept that this accumulation of damage due to earlier infection and injury of environmental origin is the sole cause of senescence. Rather, senescence is seen as an innate process which would occur even in the absence of injury and disease. Separation of the environmental and innate components of age-related deterioration is difficult, but several pieces of evidence suggest that the environmental component is not as great as might be expected. First of all, there is no evidence to suggest that the maximum human life-span in modern industrial societies is any greater than that in underdeveloped countries, or than that in previous centuries. If previous disease history is important, we might expect that the antibiotics and immunization procedures now used would reduce the damage due to disease and thus increase life-span. Average life-spans are now greater in western societies, but the maximum longevity seems not to have been changed.

A second line of evidence suggesting that disease may not be an important cause of-ageing is that provided by studies of germ-free mice and rats. The results obtained by different workers are not entirely consistent, but in general they suggest that, although the average age at death may be different, the maximum life-span is not increased in a pathogen-free environment.

Curtis and his colleagues (see Curtis, 1966) have attempted to test experimentally the idea that ageing is due to residual damage from disease and injury. They subjected mice to repeated doses of substances such as nitrogen mustard or tetanus toxin over a period of many months. When the stress was removed, they found that the animals lived as long as those which had never been treated. Thus these stresses did not appear to cause an increase in the rate of ageing. Comparable results have been obtained with *D. melanogaster* subjected to thermal stresses. However, we know that some agents, in particular sub-lethal doses of ionizing radiation, undoubtedly do affect longevity adversely (see chapter 5).

All that we can conclude from the evidence outlined above is that there is no compelling reason to believe that ageing changes are caused solely by the cumulative residual effects of disease, injury, and wear and tear. Environmental factors such as disease and injury must play some part, but it is not clear how big a part it is.

2.5   Age-related changes which improve the chances of survival

It would be a mistake to assume that all of the changes that occur as we get older are detrimental and result in an increase in the chances of dying. In man and many higher vertebrates, one very obvious beneficial effect of increased age is increased wisdom. As we get older, we gain experience and learn to avoid potentially hazardous situations. Thus, although our ability to repair damage due to injury and infection may be lower, the need to be able to repair it may also be less.

Another potentially beneficial effect of increased age is a result of our "immunological memory". As we shall discuss in chapter 6, after maturity the efficiency of the immune system declines. The body is less able to cope with new foreign substances. Yet, in spite of this, older animals may be more capable than young animals of tolerating exposure to some infections. This might be the case if they have had past experience of them, because the immunological system responds more effectively to the second exposure to an antigenic stimulus than it does to the first. Therefore, older people are less likely to contract many of the infectious diseases if they have suffered from them once already.

Another category of age-related changes which may sometimes improve the chances of survival is that associated with declining reproductive capacity. This may seem strange, since we feel intuitively that declining ability to reproduce is a typical ageing change. The menopause in a woman marks the end of her reproductive life-span and is a definite loss of functional capacity. However, in terms of many of the definitions of ageing which we have considered, it would be difficult to classify it as part of the ageing process. It does not contribute to the age-related increase in mortality. On the contrary, the menopause may enhance the chances of a woman's survival, since it means the end of the hazard of pregnancy and childbearing. It is an age-related change which illustrates how difficult it is to define ageing processes adequately and completely.

Declining reproductive ability is characteristic of ageing in both sexes in many vertebrate and invertebrate animals. Figure 2.9 shows the age-dependent decline in the number of eggs laid by the fruitfly *D. subobscura* and by the domestic fowl. In their natural environments it is unlikely that many birds or flies live long enough for any appreciable reproductive decline to occur. If they did, their chances of survival would probably be enhanced by the reduction in egg-laying. While laying eggs, the risk of attack by predators is high. Moreover, egg production is a drain on food reserves, and there is laboratory evidence showing that egg-laying does reduce the life-span of some experimental animals (see chapter 4).

In many animals, the decline in reproductive function is known to be associated with hormonal changes, structural changes, and a loss of sexual vigour. In women, oestrogen and progesterone levels fall as the numbers of ovarian follicles and functional corpora lutea decline. Pituitary

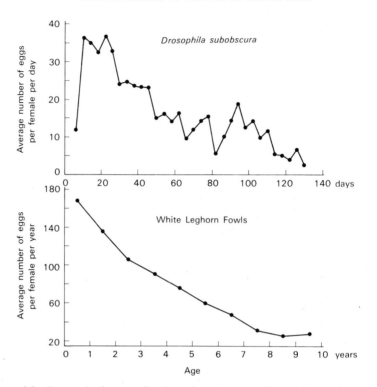

Figure 2.9 Egg production as a function of age in *Drosophila subobscura* (unpublished data) and the domestic fowl (based on data of Clark, *Poultry Science*, **19**, 61, 1940).

gonadotrophin levels increase. In association with these changes in hormone balance, there are changes in secondary sexual characteristics, such as the amount of pubic hair and the appearance of the breasts. In men, possibly as a result of changes in the number and activity of the interstitial Leydig cells in the testes, there is a gradual decrease in the secretion of androgens and an increase in gonadotrophins, beginning soon after 25 years of age. The functional activities of the accessory sex glands also decrease.

Old men and castrated men have in common features such as higher voices, weaker muscles and a tendency to have "female" characteristics. These similarities were probably responsible in part for the one-time popular belief that ageing was caused by deficiencies in the gonads, and that rejuvenation could be accomplished by injecting extracts of testes or by implanting testicular tissue into old men. There is evidence which shows that injecting sex hormones can reverse some of the effects associated with gonadal decline, but there is no evidence to suggest that the more generalized effects of senescence are in any way retarded by sex hormones. The length of life of male and female castrates is similar to that of normal people.

2.6 Conclusions

We have examined some of the age-related changes in appearance and in functional abilities which are found in man and other animals. Most systems show changes with age, although the rate at which the changes occur and the time at which particular systems show their peaks of efficiency differ. Some functions show an approximately linear decline with age after maturity, but the true relationship between age and the rate of change is difficult to ascertain without sizeable longitudinal studies.

At the beginning of this chapter we posed a question which suggested that it might be possible to measure various characteristics of individuals, and from the measurements to estimate biological age, and hence predict longevity. At present we are a long way from being able to do this. Some of the highest correlations with age are found for characters such as hair-greying and skin elasticity, but it is doubtful whether changes in these characters contribute greatly to increased mortality. Therefore, although they indicate chronological age, they may not indicate biological age at all well. Declining reproductive capacity also has a high correlation with chronological age, yet this functional change may even increase the chances of survival. It is clear that, although many of the changes which we have considered in this chapter are signs of increasing age, they are not directly responsible for the progressive increase in the probability of dying. They are symptoms and consequences of ageing processes, not the causes. The variety of age-related changes which can be seen, and the known complexity of the interactions of different cells, tissues and organ systems in the body, make it evident that studying changes in appearances and gross physiological function will give only a very crude picture of the rate at which ageing processes occur and of their cause.

C

CHAPTER THREE

AGEING AT THE POPULATION LEVEL

IT IS EASIEST TO START OUR DISCUSSION OF THE WAY IN WHICH MORTALITY statistics can be used to show that ageing changes are occurring, by considering first of all a hypothetical population made up of individuals which do not undergo senescence. We shall assume that the animals in this population are born fully mature and do not deteriorate in any way as they grow older. They are potentially immortal. We shall also assume that the only cause of death in the population is predation, and that the imaginary animals do not learn to avoid predators. Since these imaginary animals do not undergo developmental or senescent changes, to the predator a one-year-old animal is exactly the same as a hundred-year-old animal. The predator has no way of distinguishing between them, so they are both equally likely to be caught. The final assumptions that we shall make are that the

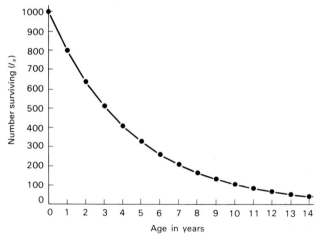

Figure 3.1 A survival curve for a population of individuals which do not undergo senescence.

Table 3.1 Life-table for a hypothetical population which does not show ageing.

x years	l_x	d_x	q_x	e_x
0 – 1	1000	200	0.2	5
1 – 2	800	160	0.2	5
2 – 3	640	128	0.2	5
3 – 4	512	102	0.2	5
4 – 5	410	82	0.2	5
5 – 6	328	66	0.2	5
6 – 7	262	52	0.2	5
7 – 8	210	42	0.2	5
8 – 9	168	34	0.2	5
9 – 10	134	27	0.2	5
10 – 11	107	21	0.2	5
11 – 12	86	17	0.2	5
12 – 13	69	14	0.2	5
13 – 14	55	11	0.2	5
14 – 15	44	9	0.2	5
15 – 16	35	7	0.2	5
:	:	:	:	:
:	:	:	:	:

death rate due to predation is 20% a year, and that the birth rate is such as to replace exactly the number lost by predation. If we marked 1000 animals at birth and followed them throughout life, recording the time at which each was killed, how many would still be alive after 10 years? What would be the average life-span of the animals in the population?

Table 3.1 is the first part of a life-table for such a hypothetical population. A life-table is simply a concise summary of the statistics of survival and death in relation to age. The symbols used in Table 3.1 are those which are conventionally used in the study of human and animal populations. For every age interval, x, the life-table gives l_x, the number of animals alive at the beginning of that interval. The original sample of animals on which the life-table is based is referred to as the *cohort*. In our example the cohort is 1000 imaginary animals and the age interval used is one year. The column l_x therefore starts at 1000 and would, if the life-table was complete, end at 0.

Survival data like those shown in column l_x are frequently plotted to give a survival curve such as is shown in figure 3.1. As can be seen, the curve for this particular population is a typical exponential die-away curve.

All of the remaining information in the life-table can be derived from l_x, and l_x could be derived from any of the other columns in the table. The third column d_x gives the number of animals dying during each age interval.

$$d_x = l_x - l_{(x+1)}$$

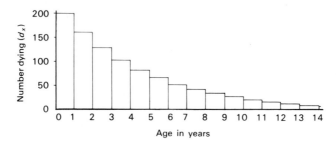

Figure 3.2 Distribution of the ages at death of individuals in a population of animals which do not undergo senescence.

Figure 3.2 shows the way in which the number of animals dying in each age interval changes with age. The number dying declines with age simply because, with the passage of time, there are fewer animals left to die.

A rather more useful and important way of measuring the rate of death is given in the column headed q_x which is the age-specific death rate. It is the proportion of the animals alive at the beginning of the age interval that die during that interval. In other words, it is the chance of dying during any year.

$$q_x \;=\; \frac{d_x}{l_x}$$

We have said that in our imaginary population 20% of the animals are killed by predation every year, so obviously at all ages $q_x = 0.2$. The age-specific death rate is plotted against age in figure 3.3 and is, of course, a straight line parallel to the age axis, showing that the age-specific death rate is constant.

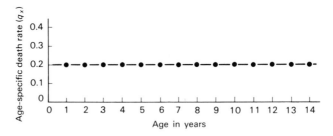

Figure 3.3 Age-specific death rate in a population of animals which do not undergo senescence.

If the age intervals are very small and the population is large, the age-specific death rate is approximately the same as the force of mortality μ_x.

$$\mu_x = - \frac{1}{l_x} \cdot \frac{dl_x}{dx}$$

Frequently the terms *force of mortality* and *age-specific death rate* are used interchangeably.

The last column, e_x, is the mean further expectation of life at the beginning of the age interval x. At age 0 it is the mean length of life for the cohort. It is obtained by dividing the total number of animal-years to be lived by the population by the number of animals available to live them. Strictly speaking it is the area under the survival curve beyond age x divided by the number of survivors at that age:

$$e_x = \frac{\int_x^w l_x \, dx}{l_x}$$

where w is the last age in the complete life-table. For our hypothetical population it is easy to estimate e_x. It is approximately $1/q_x$ which is 5 years at all ages. However, as will be described in the next section, for real populations e_x is usually calculated from the life-table itself.

Before going on to consider life-tables for human and other animal populations, let us summarize the characteristics of our hypothetical population which does not show senescence:

(i) As the survival curve shows, the number surviving is a decreasing exponential function of time.
(ii) The further expectation of life is constant at all ages.
(iii) The age-specific death rate or force of mortality is constant at all ages.

3.1 The life-table of a laboratory population

The life-table characteristics of most laboratory populations are very different from those of our hypothetical population of potentially immortal animals. Table 3.2 shows a life-table for a cohort of 750 adult male *Drosophila melanogaster* reared and maintained under carefully controlled laboratory conditions. The raw data consisted of the number of flies dying in each 4-day interval. It will be noted that the l_x value in the table is 1000, although the actual cohort was only 750. It is a common convention to stan-

Table 3.2 Life-table for adult male *Drosophila melanogaster*

x days	l_x	d_x	q_x	L_x	T_x	e_x
0 – 4	1000	0	0	1000.0	11864.0	47.5
4 – 8	1000	1	0.001	999.5	10864.0	43.5
8 – 12	999	4	0.004	997.0	9864.5	39.5
12 – 16	995	7	0.007	991.5	8867.5	35.6
16 – 20	988	5	0.005	985.5	7876.0	31.9
20 – 24	983	7	0.007	979.5	6890.5	28.0
24 – 28	976	17	0.017	967.5	5911.0	24.2
28 – 32	959	23	0.024	947.5	4943.5	20.6
32 – 36	936	72	0.077	900.0	3996.0	17.1
36 – 40	864	116	0.134	806.0	3096.0	14.3
40 – 44	748	178	0.238	659.0	2290.0	12.2
44 – 48	570	125	0.219	507.5	1631.0	11.4
48 – 52	445	107	0.240	391.5	1123.5	10.1
52 – 56	338	111	0.328	282.5	732.0	8.7
56 – 60	227	83	0.366	185.5	449.5	7.9
60 – 64	144	39	0.271	124.5	264.0	7.3
64 – 68	105	51	0.486	79.5	139.5	5.3
68 – 72	54	29	0.537	39.5	60.0	4.4
72 – 76	25	17	0.680	16.5	20.5	3.3
76 – 80	8	8	1.000	4.0	4.0	2.0
80 – 84	0	–	–	–	–	–

dardize life-tables by applying a scaling factor so that l_x is always 1000 or, for human populations, 100 000. For the *Drosophila* population, the raw data for the number dead at each age were simply multiplied by 1000/750 to obtain the data in the d_x column, and all the subsequent calculations were based on the scaled d_x values. Although this standardization is useful because it makes comparisons between different sets of data much easier, it does have the disadvantage that it may, when the actual cohort is small, give a misleading impression of the accuracy of the life-table.

There are two additional columns, L_x and T_x, in the life-table represented in Table 3.2. These two quantities are needed in order to calculate the further expectation of life. They were not necessary with the hypothetical population, where the survival curve was a smooth exponential, and it was therefore easy to calculate the areas under the curve. With real populations where the death rate is changing all the time, this calculation is more difficult. The age structure L_x is the average number of animals alive during the age interval x:

$$L_x = \int_{x}^{x+l} l_x \, dx$$

However, for relatively small age intervals, L_x is usually approximated by taking the average of the numbers alive at the beginning and end of the age interval:

$$L_x = \frac{l_x + l_{(x+1)}}{2}$$

The total number of animal-age-units to be lived by animals alive at the beginning of the age interval x, T_x, is then approximated by:

$$T_x = L_x + L_{(x+1)} + L_{(x+2)} \quad \text{........} \quad + L_w$$

$$= \sum_{x}^{w} L_x$$

Multiplying this value by the size of the age interval a gives an approximation of the area under the curve beyond the beginning of the interval x, i.e. the total number of fly-days to be lived by the flies alive at the beginning of interval x. The further expectation of life at the beginning of age interval x is then:

$$e_x = \frac{T_x\, a}{l_x}$$

It is worth pointing out at this stage that e_o, the further expectation of life at birth, is not what is usually meant by the "life-span" of an animal. The term *life-span* is not very precise, but generally it is used for a rather vague "mean maximum" age to which an animal may live. For example, the life-span of man is traditionally "three-score years and ten" but, in many underdeveloped countries, high infant and childhood mortality mean that at birth e_o, the average expectation of life, is only about 40 years. "Life-span" tends to refer to the age that may be achieved by some members of the population, not the average expectation of life of all the individuals in it. The life-span of our hypothetical population is indeterminate; a "mean maximum" life-span cannot be given.

The *Drosophila* life-table data are shown graphically in figure 3.4. The survival curve is a typical "rectangular" curve which is characteristic for animals which show senescence. During the first 30 days of life very few flies die, but thereafter the number dying increases rapidly. The number of deaths in each age interval increases and then decreases, since as the cohort ages the number of survivors decreases and therefore the number of deaths in each age interval must also fall. However, as the third part of the figure

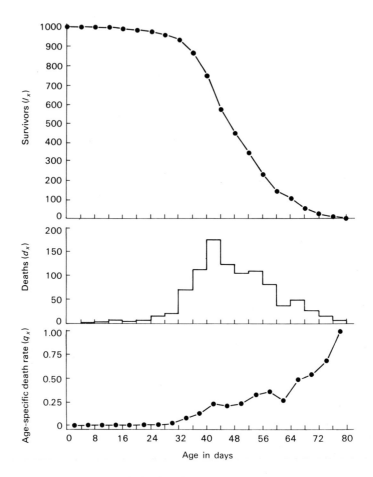

Figure 3.4 Survival curve, distribution of ages at death, and age-specific death rate for a population of male *Drosophila melanogaster*.

shows, the age-specific death rate increases fairly steadily with time. In other words, the chances of dying increase with age.

It can be seen that the *Drosophila* life-table differs markedly from that of our hypothetical population of potentially immortal animals where the probability of death is independent of age. In contrast to the non-senescing population, the life-table for *Drosophila*, like that of most laboratory animals, shows evidence of senescence in that

(i) the survival curve is rectangular in shape,
(ii) the further expectation of life decreases with increasing age,
(iii) the age-specific death rate increases with age.

The two life-tables that we have considered so far are two extreme types, one with all deaths due to random age-independent causes, and the other with mortality concentrated in old age. Many life-tables show an intermediate situation, with the survival curve more or less diagonal, showing a constant number of deaths per unit time. There is also a third theoretically possible extreme type of life-table: one where there is a high age-specific death rate in early life followed by a lower rate later in life. The survival curves for such populations tend to be L-shaped. If it was possible to obtain the data, the survival curves for many wild populations of, for example, fish and other animals where there is a very high juvenile mortality would probably be of this type. Indeed if instead of considering adult flies we had started our life-table for *Drosophila* with a cohort of larvae, the high mortality which usually occurs in the larval and pupal stages would have resulted in an initial decrease in the force of mortality with age. As we shall see in the next section, human survival curves also start with an initial sharp decline in the number of survivors.

3.2 The life-tables of human populations

For each of the life-tables that we have discussed so far, the data were obtained by taking a cohort of animals born at the same time and recording the age at death of each individual. This type of life-table is known as a *cohort, dynamic, age-specific* or *horizontal* life-table. Since it is based directly on the fate of a real cohort, we shall refer to it as a *cohort life-table*.

It is impracticable to use this method of obtaining the data with human and many animal populations, because it is not possible to keep track of all the individuals throughout their lives. Life-tables for human populations are therefore constructed by rather different methods, and are known as *indirect, static, time-specific* or *vertical* life-tables. They are based on the age structure of a population at a point in time. Since they describe the method of obtaining the data, we shall refer to them as *indirect life-tables*. As we shall see later, there are important differences between the two types of life-table. These differences are essentially the same as those between longitudinal and cross-sectional studies of age-related changes.

The precise methods used in the construction of human life-tables are complex, and a detailed description of them is not necessary for our purposes, so only an outline of the basic computations will be given. The raw

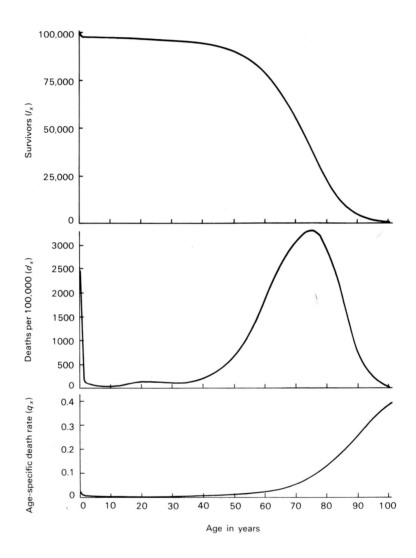

Figure 3.5 Survival curve, distribution of ages at death, and age-specific death rate for human males (based on the English Life Table No. 12, 1960–1962).

material comes from two sources, census data and death certificates. Census data give the size of the population and the number of people of different ages in it; death certificates for the same period provide the information about the number and age of the people who die in the year of the census. Combining the two sets of data enables q_x, the age-specific death rate, to be calculated for each age group. It is then assumed that there is a theoretical cohort of 100 000 people and that the age-specific death rate for each successive age interval acts on that cohort.

Figure 3.5 shows the survival curve, mortality and force-of-mortality curves based on a life-table for human males calculated in a way similar to that described above. Apart from the fairly high mortality during infancy, the curves are very similar to, although much smoother than, those for the laboratory *Drosophila* cohort. The human life-table is based on very large numbers.

It is important to realize that this indirect type of life-table is very different from the cohort life-table. The latter gives a true historical account of an actual population. For example, for a human cohort born in 1900, a cohort life-table would give the age-specific death rate which existed for 1-year-olds in 1901, 2-year-olds in 1902, 3-year-olds in 1903, and so on. It could not be completed, since many of the people born in 1900 are still alive. In contrast to this, the indirect life-table which is more usual for humans gives an instantaneous picture of the mortality statistics of a hypothetical population at the time when the data were collected. For the 1961 census, the age-specific death rates in the life-table are those for 1-year-olds, 2-year-olds, 3-year-olds, etc., in 1961. The two types of life-table will be the same only if the age structure of the population and the environmental conditions are constant over long periods of time. For human populations they certainly have not been constant. Table 3.3 shows the way in which the force of mortality at various ages has changed during the past half-century. There

Table 3.3 Secular changes in the force of mortality at various ages for English males (based on the Registrar General's Decennial Supplement, 1961).

Age (years)	Years				
	1910 – 12	1920 – 22	1930 – 32	1950 – 52	1960 – 62
0	0.12044	0.08996	0.07186	0.03266	0.02449
10	0.00193	0.00181	0.00146	0.00052	0.00039
20	0.00348	0.00349	0.00316	0.00129	0.00119
40	0.00811	0.00688	0.00562	0.00290	0.00235
60	0.03042	0.02561	0.02415	0.02369	0.02287
80	0.14299	0.14002	0.14500	0.13629	0.12747

has been a striking reduction in the force of mortality in the post-natal period, presumably as a result of better nutrition, sanitation and medical care. Therefore the survival curve for any real cohort which could be completed at the present time would show a much higher force of mortality in early years of life than that shown in figure 3.5, since the cohort would have been born before the improvement in health care.

3.3   Life-tables for natural populations of animals

It is extremely difficult to obtain accurate life-tables for natural populations in the wild. In theory, the easiest method of getting the data is to mark a cohort of individuals at birth, and then record either the time when each dies, or the number remaining alive at suitable time-intervals. Marking a cohort may be easy, but knowing the time of death is often very difficult. For example, if predators are a cause of death, the predator may completely eat the carcass or remove it from the site, so that the death can only be recorded if it was actually observed. Similarly, direct observation of the number of marked individuals alive at different times is difficult unless the animals are sessile, since it is impossible to know whether a reduction in numbers is due to death or to migration from the area. Nevertheless, in spite of the difficulties, ecologists have developed techniques which have permitted cohort life-tables to be constructed for a number of different species.

Figure 3.6 shows the survival curve for wild lapwings. It is based on

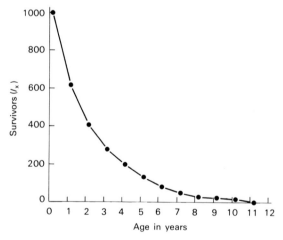

Figure 3.6   A survival curve for lapwings (*Vanellus vanellus*) based on 460 birds banded as nestlings (data from Lack, *British Birds*, **36**, 214, 1943).

recoveries of birds banded as nestlings and is very similar to that of our hypothetical population of non-senescent animals. The survival curve is exponential, the further expectation of life is constant at between 2.2 and 2.6 years, and the age-specific death rate does not change substantially for the first nine years. Thereafter the number of survivors is so small that the estimates of e_x and q_x are in any case very unreliable. Most life-tables for wild birds show these characteristics, the characteristics which we have said are those of populations of animals which do not undergo senescent changes. Does this mean that birds are not subject to age-related deterioration? The answer to this question must be no. In captivity, birds have been found to have quite a high average expectation of life, usually more than ten years. The reason for the exponential type of survival curve found for wild populations is almost certainly that the death rate from predation and other causes is so great that senescence has no opportunity to show itself – almost all members of the cohort are dead before any significant decline in vitality has occurred. A very large birth cohort would be needed in order to demonstrate a significant change in the force of mortality with increase in age.

With some animals the collection of life-table data is made easier by the fact that the age of individuals can be estimated directly. For example, fish age can be assessed by counting the annual growth rings on the scales or in the otiliths; some ungulates can be aged from growth rings in the horns, and the shells of some molluscs also have annual growth rings. If a large random sample can be obtained from a population where individual ages can be deduced from growth rings, then providing the population is a stationary one with the number of animals joining each age class being exactly the same as the number lost by death, the age distribution of the sample will enable an indirect life-table to be constructed. Sometimes data from hunting records provide the basis for life-tables such as these. Figure 3.7 shows the survival curve for Dall mountain sheep. It is based on a collection of 608 skulls of animals which were assumed to have been killed by wolves. Since the skulls of young animals are probably more perishable than those of other age groups, it is likely that they were under-represented in the sample, and hence the death rate in the first few months of life is underestimated. Nevertheless, the survival curve shows definite evidence of senescence. It is in fact very similar to that for human populations, with high juvenile mortality followed by a plateau with very few deaths and then a rapid decline in the number left alive.

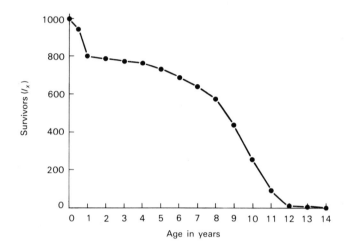

Figure 3.7 A survival curve for Dall Mountain Sheep based on 608 sheep whose age at death was determined from annual growth rings on the horns (based on data of Murie, given in Deevey, 1947).

3.4 Life-tables and ageing

Gerontologists are interested in life-tables because age-mortality relationships may show whether or not senescence is taking place in the individuals in a population. It is assumed that deterioration in individuals will show itself by an increased vulnerability, and therefore by a progressive increase in the age-specific death rate in the population. However, it must be remembered that ageing is a gradual process occurring in individuals, whereas life-tables are based on the distribution in the population of the single event death. How much, or how little, can we deduce about ageing processes from the time of death? Is a progressive increase in the force of mortality always necessarily an indication that senescence is taking place in individuals? Does the rate of change in the force of mortality have any relation to the rate of ageing?

We have already suggested that, although the survival curve of a wild lapwing population superficially resembles that of a population of non-senescent individuals, to infer from this that lapwings do not undergo senescence would be mistaken. They do undergo senescent changes, but normally in the wild mortality is so high that senescence is unlikely to be observed, because almost all the birds die before any age-related deterioration becomes pronounced. It is also possible to imagine situations where a typical rectangular survival curve might be an equally misleading indication that senescent changes are occurring when actually they are not. An increase in the force of mortality with age is evidence of increasing vulnerability if, and only if, the causes of death are random in their incidence, i.e. if all individuals are equally at risk at all ages. It is easy to think of circumstances in which this would not be true. A situation where young animals are protected from hazards to which older animals are exposed would inevitably lead to an increase in the force of mortality, irrespective of any ageing processes. In many countries only men above the age of 18 are liable to be called up for military service. Therefore, even if human beings did not show developmental or ageing changes, in times of war the force of mortality for men would be higher in the age groups above 18 than in those below this age. In fact the English Life-Table for 1960–62 shows that, whereas the force of mortality for females increases steadily after the age of 11, for males it increases up to the age of 20, then falls slightly until it reaches a minimum at 26 before beginning to increase again. This small peak in the force of mortality in youth is presumably associated with the fact that young men are more likely than other groups to put themselves in a situation where there is a high risk of accidents occurring.

An age-related increase in the force of mortality may also be a misleading indication that senescent changes are occurring if there are secular changes in the risks to which individuals are exposed. We have already touched on this problem while discussing human life-tables, where it is apparent that, thanks to antibiotics, immunization, improved public health, etc., there has been a decrease during the past half-century in the hazards to which individuals are exposed. For animal populations it is not difficult to think of cases where risks might increase with time. If a cohort is being followed from birth to death, an increase in the force of mortality is an indication of senescence only if the environmental conditions have not become more severe. A bad winter, or the introduction into the area of a new predator or competitor, would increase the death rate even in the absence of senescence. In order to compensate to some extent for inevitable secular changes, ecologists usually try to follow several different birth cohorts when they are collecting data for life-tables.

Since, in spite of the difficulties which have just been considered, a progressive increase in the force of mortality can usually be used as evidence that senescence is occurring in individuals, it is natural (but unwise) to think that the rates of increase in the force of mortality in populations reflect the rates of ageing in the individuals in them. More than a century and a half ago Gompertz showed that the age-specific death rate or force of mortality for humans beyond the age of about 35 increases exponentially with age:

$$\mu_x = A e^{\alpha x}$$

where A is the intercept, a hypothetical value for the force of mortality at birth, and α is the slope constant. When the logarithm of the age-specific mortality rate is plotted against age, it therefore shows a linear relationship for part of the life-span. Many life-tables for laboratory animals show this "Gompertz relationship". Typical Gompertz plots for the human and *Drosophila* life-tables discussed earlier are shown in figure 3.8. It has also been found that Gompertz plots of death rates from specific causes such as hypertension, hernia, neoplasia, etc., are also linear for at least a substantial part of the life-span.

The simple Gompertz equation has been modified a number of times in order to improve the fit to the observed data. For example, Makeham suggested that the relationship was improved by including an additive constant B, reflecting age-independent causes of death:

$$\mu_x = A e^{\alpha x} + B$$

Other modifications have been made which improve the relationship at both extreme young and old ages, where the Gompertz or Gompertz-Makeham equations do not adequately describe the data for human populations.

The exponential increase in the force of mortality which the Gompertz equation and its modifications describe, does not mean that the rate of ageing increases exponentially. Strehler (1962) has shown how a number of mathematical models relating ageing processes to mortality statistics all predict the Gompertz relationship. These models include some in which the decline in physiological function is assumed to be a linear or decreasing function of time, as well as those in which it increases.

Not only is it wrong to assume that an exponential increase in the force of mortality reflects a logarithmic increase in the rate at which ageing processes are occurring, it is also wrong to assume that differences in the slope or intercept of the Gompertz equations for different populations necessarily reflect differences in the rate of ageing in those populations. If the force of mortality begins to increase earlier in one population than in another, it may simply mean that the environmental conditions are harsher in the former than in the latter. The amount of genetic heterogeneity in a population will also affect the rate of increase in the force of mortality. A

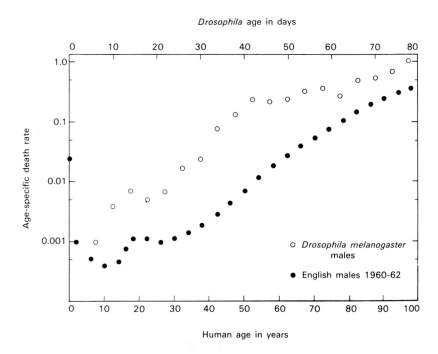

Figure 3.8 Gompertz plots for man and male *Drosophila melanogaster*.

genetically uniform population would be expected to give a very rectangular survival curve and show a rapid increase in the force of mortality. A less uniform population, in which some individuals were weaker at birth than others, would give a less-rectangular survival curve. The force of mortality would increase more slowly, but this would not mean that the rate of ageing is different from that in a genetically-uniform population.

Life-table data and the relationship between the force of mortality and age which they show may, therefore, enable us to say whether or not ageing changes are occurring, but they can provide only a very limited amount of information about the rate at which ageing processes are occurring in the individuals in a population. Nevertheless, any theories which attempt to explain ageing processes must be compatible with the mortality statistics shown in life-tables.

D

3.5   The evolution of senescence

One of the problems which has intrigued biologists for many years is why senescence should occur at all. As Williams (1957) wrote:

It is indeed remarkable that after a seemingly miraculous feat of morphogenesis, a complex metazoan should be unable to perform the much simpler task of merely maintaining what is already formed.

There have been a number of hypotheses attempting to explain the existence of senescence in evolutionary terms. The starting point of the most widely accepted of these is the fact that we discussed in the first part of this chapter, namely that death is inevitable, even in populations of individuals which do not undergo senescent changes, and that with increasing age fewer and fewer animals are left alive. From this starting point Williams (1957) and Medawar (1952) developed rather similar hypotheses. They suggested that senescence is an inevitable but mainly indirect consequence of natural selection.

At first sight it seems obvious that natural selection will always tend to increase life-span and will never favour senescence. The longer an animal lives the more offspring it is likely to produce, and therefore the greater the chances of its genes, including those which are responsible for the long life-span, spreading through the population. However, this argument, although basically correct, makes no allowance for the fact that even in the complete absence of senescence, at birth the chances that an animal will actually produce offspring at an advanced age are very small, simply because it is most unlikely that it will live that long. Medawar and Williams pointed out that the important consequence of this is that selection against genes which have potentially deleterious effects late in life will be very weak. A gene which results in the death of a wild bird at one year of age will be selected against; that bird will not have reproduced, and hence the gene cannot be passed on to the next generation. On the other hand, a gene which results in death at 20 years of age will be relatively unimportant; a wild bird is most unlikely to live that long and, if it does, it will already have made a substantial contribution to the next generation. The average number of offspring left by non-senescing birds will be only slightly more than the average number of offspring produced by birds with genes which could cause their death at 20 years of age. A deleterious gene will therefore tend to remain in the population if its effects become apparent late enough in life.

Selection will always tend to postpone the time when deleterious genetic effects appear since, if they appear late enough, it is effectively the same as eliminating the genes which cause them. If a gene produces a detrimental effect which shows an early age of onset in some individuals and a late age of onset in others, and if the differences in the age of onset are themselves determined genetically by modifying genes, then selection will favour late onset. In other words selection will tend to increase longevity. Eventually, however, the force of natural selection becomes so small that it can advance the age of onset no further.

Williams has stressed the effect that the reduction in the force of natural selection with age will have on the selection of a gene which has pleiotropic effects, that is to say on a gene which affects more than one aspect of the phenotype. It is well known that most mutant genes which occur in laboratory populations have several phenotypic effects, and not infrequently the various effects become apparent at different stages of the life history. If such a gene has a favourable effect early in life, for example by increasing fertility, and another effect late in life which results in a physiological deterioration making the animal more likely to be killed, then usually the gene will spread through the population. The favourable effect in youth will result in more offspring being produced by many of the animals which carry the gene, whereas the effect late in life is unimportant for most of the carriers of the gene, because they die from accidental causes before the late genetic effect shows itself. Selection will therefore always tend to favour vigour in youth, even if it is at the expense of a deleterious effect later in life. Once a gene of the type that we are considering becomes established in a population it will mean that the chances of living to an advanced age are decreased even further. Therefore other genes with similar favourable effects in youth, and adverse effects in later years, are even more likely to spread through the population.

According to the hypotheses which we have discussed, the characteristic life-span of a species will be determined by the result of a balance between direct selection tending to postpone the time of action of deleterious genetic effects, and the indirect effect of selection of genes which give improved fitness early in life at the expense of greater vulnerability later on. Hamilton (1966) has used a mathematical model to investigate how the age at which a gene acts influences its effect on fitness, and has reached conclusions which agree with and extend the basic ideas of Medawar and Williams. He showed that senescence is an inevitable result of the working of natural selection, and suggests that higher fertility will be one of the main factors leading to a high rate of senescence.

One of the important implications of these ideas about the evolution of senescence is that we should expect many causes of ageing, not a single one.

Senescence will be the result of natural selection pushing all the deleterious genetic effects towards an age which few individuals ever reach. The tendency for a number of different tissues and organs to show senescent changes at the same time is not necessarily due to their functional interdependence, or to the existence of a single common "ageing factor" in all of them. It could simply be due to the fact that natural selection has tended to synchronize the time of expression of many independent deleterious genetic effects.

An alternative, although probably less generally accepted, hypothesis concerning the evolution of senescence has been discussed in general terms by Wynne–Edwards (1962). He suggested that senescence is a result of direct selection for a limited life-span, because a limited life-span favours group survival. For the group, in contrast to the individual, long life-spans are not necessarily advantageous. In order for a group to survive in a changing environment, it may have to change genetically. If the environmental conditions are changing rapidly, then the group may become extinct unless it too can change rapidly. Since a particular area can support only a limited population, a short life-span may be advantageous, because it will allow relatively more generations in a given time. The more rapid the turnover of individuals, the more different gene combinations there will be for natural selection to act on, and therefore the greater the chances of the group adapting rapidly enough to survive in a changing environment. Groups with long individual life-spans will not be able to evolve as quickly as groups with a shorter average life-span. Senescence is therefore a favourable group characteristic which, providing it is accompanied by appropriate reproductive rates, enhances the chances that the group will survive. The characteristic length of life will be determined by selection between groups and will depend on many aspects of the biology of the species. Wynne-Edwards pointed out that some of the most successful animals in terms of numbers of species are the insects, the rodents among the mammals, the Passeres among the birds; and all of these have relatively short life-spans. It could be that their short life-spans have contributed to their success.

The main criticism which is made of Wynne–Edwards's ideas about the direct selective advantage of senescence is that it is difficult to see how the advantage of senescence to the group can outweigh the selective disadvantage to the individual. Providing that there is no loss of fertility with age, direct selection will always tend to favour longer life-spans as far as individuals are concerned, since longer life-spans result in the production of more offspring.

Even if Wynne–Edwards is correct in thinking that senescence evolved through group selection, it would still not lead us to expect a single cause of ageing. Presumably selection would result in many different genetic changes which would cause a limited life-span.

CHAPTER FOUR

THE LENGTH OF LIFE

IN SPITE OF THE DIFFICULTY OF OBTAINING ADEQUATE LIFE-TABLE DATA FOR
most animals, enough is known about the longevity of the various species to
make it quite clear that one of the most important facts which any generalized theory of ageing must be capable of explaining is that different species
have different characteristic life-spans. In this chapter we shall survey briefly
some of the data which show the wide range of life-spans found in different
groups of animals, and then go on to consider the extent to which the
differences in longevity found within a species are due to hereditary factors.

4.1 The life-span of mammals

Table 4.1 gives the maximum recorded life-span of a number of common
mammals. The data are taken from the *Biology Data Book* (1972) which
gives a far more extensive list than that given in the table, and also gives the
source of the longevity record for each species. Before discussing the data it
is necessary to consider how representative of the true longevity potential of
each species the figures are likely to be. The life-span given is the maximum
length of life recorded for animals kept in captivity in zoos or laboratories,
or as farm animals or domestic pets. This means that many of the figures
are based on very small samples. The longevities of many thousands of
laboratory mice and domestic cats have been recorded, so the figures given
are probably a reasonably good indication of the maximum life-spans of
these species. On the other hand, the numbers of brown bears or porcupines
which have been kept in captivity are relatively small, and the figures given
may not be at all representative of the maximum longevity attainable. The
more animals that have been kept in captivity, the greater the maximum
recorded longevity is likely to be, simply because large samples are more
likely to include a potentially long-lived individual than small samples. There
is another reason why the longevity records of animals which are not commonly kept in captivity may be relatively low: the more individuals of a

Table 4.1 Maximum recorded life-spans for mammals kept in captivity (based on data from *Biology Data Book*, Vol. 1, 1972)

Species	Common name	Maximum life-span
Order Artiodactyla		
Capra hircus	wild goat	18 y
Camelus bactrianus	Bactrian camel	29 y 5 mo
Hippopotamus amphibius	hippopotamus	51 y
Order Perissodactyla		
Tapirus terrestris	South American tapir	30 y 5 mo
Equus caballus	domestic horse	46 y
Rhinoceros unicornis	Indian rhinoceros	40 y
Order Proboscidea		
Elephas maximus	Indian elephant	70 y
Order Tubulidentata		
Orycteropus afer	aardvark	12 y
Order Pinnipedia		
Phoca vitulina	harbour or common seal	>34 y
Order Carnivora		
Canis familiaris	dog	20 y
Felis catus	domestic cat	28 y
Ursus arctos	brown bear	36 y 10 mo
Mustela vison	American mink	10 y
Order Rodentia		
Cavia porcellus	guinea pig	7 y 6 mo
Hystrix brachyura	porcupine	27 y 3 mo
Mus musculus	house mouse	3 y 6 mo
Rattus rattus	black rat	4 y 8 mo
Order Lagomorpha		
Oryctolagus cuniculus	European rabbit	13 y
Order Edentata		
Dasypus novemcinctus	nine-banded armadillo	10 y 4 mo
Order Primates		
Galago crassicaudatus	thick-tailed bush baby	14 y
Cebus capucinus	white-throated capuchin monkey	>40 y
Gorilla gorilla	gorilla	>39 y 4 mo
Pan troglodytes	chimpanzee	>44 y 6 mo
Pongo pygmaeus	orang-utan	>50 y

Table 4.1 *continued over page*

Table 4.1 *continued*

Species	Common name	Maximum life-span
Order Chiroptera		
Eidolon helvum	African fruit bat	21 y 10 mo
Order Insectivora		
Erinaceus europaeus	hedgehog	4 y 2 mo
Sorex palustris	Northern water shrew	1 y 6 mo
Order Marsupialia		
Macropus robustus	wallaroo or euro	19 y 7 mo
Order Monotremata		
Tachyglossus aculeatus	Australian echidna	49 y 5 mo
Ornithorhynchus anatinus	platypus	17 y

y = years   mo = months

species that are kept in captivity, the more adept human beings become at keeping them. With experience, we understand the species' environmental requirements more thoroughly, and are likely to be able to cure minor illnesses. Thus the figures which are given in the table are probably only a very crude indication of the maximum longevity for many species. Nevertheless, they do show how very different the life-span of different species can be.

Since there is so much variation in the life-spans of mammals, it is natural to look for reasons for the differences between species. Is there any structural or functional characteristic of the long-lived species which is not shared by the short-lived species? One of the things which is apparent from the table is that in general the larger mammals tend to have the longer life-spans. The possible significance of this relationship was realized by Rubner in 1908. He found that for five species of domestic mammals with very different life-spans and body weights, the total basal energy expenditure during the life-span was approximately constant at about 200 kilocalories per gram of body weight (840 J/kg. In other words, high metabolic rate was associated with short life-span and *vice versa*. The relation between size and longevity is brought about by the fact that there is a strong correlation between basal metabolic rate and size − small animals have high metabolic rates. Rubner found that although his hypothesis (that longevity was determined by metabolic rate, which in turn depended on size) seemed to hold for the five species of domestic animals for which he had data, man did not fit the general pattern. Man's lifetime energy expenditure was three times higher than that of other animals; he seemed to live too long for his size.

The relation between body size and longevity was re-examined by Sacher (1959) using data for 63 species of terrestrial placental mammals. In figure 4.1 Sacher's data for both body weight and maximum recorded life-span are plotted on a logarithmic scale. It can be seen that there is a clear correlation between the two variables. However, there are certain peculiarities apparent in the figure. First of all, as with Rubner's data, man is an exception. The value for the life-span of man seems to be more than three times greater than would be expected from his body weight; on the basis of the regression line shown in the figure, man should have a life-span of only about 30 years.

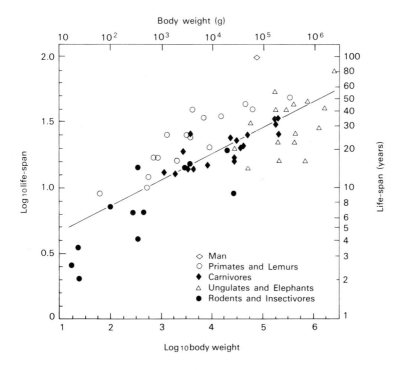

Figure 4.1 Relation of life-span to body weight for different species of mammals (redrawn from Sacher, 1959).

Secondly, there is a marked tendency for all the primates to have life-spans which are too long (the points cluster above the line), and for the rodents to have life-spans which are too short (the points cluster below the line).

Since there is a good but imperfect correlation between body weight and longevity, the next question which was asked was whether a better correlation would be obtained if the weight of some part of the body rather than total body weight was compared with longevity. Most organs of the body show a close correlation with total body weight, but one exception is the brain. For example, it is well known that primates have a relatively larger brain than rodents. In fact brain weight can vary as much as fifteen-fold for animals of the same size. The graph obtained by Sacher when he plotted log brain weight against log life-span is shown in figure 4.2. The scatter of the

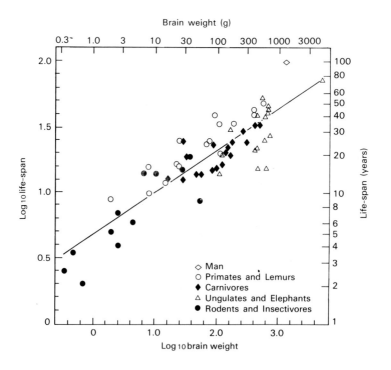

Figure 4.2 Relation of life-span to brain weight for different species of mammals (redrawn from Sacher, 1959).

points around the regression line is rather less than in figure 4.1. As the figure suggests, brain weight was found to be a better predictor of life-span than body weight. However, the best prediction of life-span was obtained by taking both body weight and brain weight into consideration, as is shown in figure 4.3. The regression line shown in the figure is based on the equation:

$$x \;=\; 0.636w \;+\; 0.198y \;+\; 0.471$$

where $x = $ log life-span, $y = $ log body weight, and $w = $ log (brain weight/body weight$^{2/3}$). The term w is known as the *index of cephalization* and is a measurement of relative brain size. As the figure shows, when both body weight and index of cephalization are taken into account, there is no longer a clustering of the points for rodents below the line and for primates above it. The observed life-span for man is that appropriate for an animal of his weight with such a relatively large brain.

Sacher has also examined the relation between brain weight, body weight and longevity within different orders of mammals. In general, the data confirmed the hypothesis that length of life is an increasing function of brain size when body size is held constant. One interesting exception to the general pattern was found with the order Chiroptera, the bats, which have life-spans of up to 20 years. This is about three times as long as would be expected on the basis of their brain and body weights. In order to understand the significance of this finding it is necessary to consider the possible explanations of the correlation shown in figure 4.3. Sacher suggested that the body-weight term is important because metabolic rate is negatively correlated with body weight. Since metabolic errors are inevitable and increase the probability of dying, large animals will, because of their lower metabolic rates, have a lower incidence of metabolic errors and hence longer life-spans than small animals. According to Sacher, the brain size of an animal is important because animals with larger brains have superior homeostatic regulatory mechanisms. If a metabolic error causes the internal environment to fluctuate away from the optimum, the likelihood of this resulting in an irreversible change leading to death will be lower in animals with good regulatory mechanisms. Thus for animals of comparable size, the potential metabolic-error rates are similar, but the animal with the larger brain will live longer because its superior homeostatic control mechanisms minimize the effects of any fluctuations away from the normal levels. If Sacher's interpretation of the body weight – brain weight – life-span relation is correct, then the fact that bats do not show the same relation as other mammals is not surprising. Most bats have a period of diurnal torpor and also a period

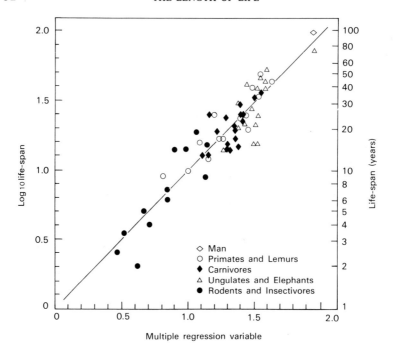

Figure 4.3   Relation of life-span to a combination of body weight and brain weight (redrawn from Sacher, 1959).

of hibernation which lasts for several months. During torpor and hibernation the metabolic rate is lower. Therefore, if longevity is inversely related to
metabolic rate, they would be expected to live longer than mammals of comparable size and brain weight.

Sacher's hypothesis provides an explanation for the differences in the
life-spans of different species. Does it help to explain the longevity
differences found within a species? When Storer (1967) looked at the brain
weight, body weight, metabolic rate and life-span of 18 different strains of
mice to see whether the relation that Sacher found between species also held
within species, he found that it did not. Indeed he found that the metabolic
rate was higher in the long-lived strains.

Although Sacher's hypothesis is attractive, it is not the only possible explanation of the observed relation between brain weight and longevity in
mammals. An alternative interpretation of the correlation is that natural
selection for long life and large brain size have gone together. For example,
it has been argued that natural selection will favour increased brain size in

potentially long-lived species, because large-brained animals have a greater learning capacity than small-brained animals. An animal that can learn by experience is more likely to survive to old age than one which does not. Therefore selection pressures which favour increased longevity will also lead to increased brain size, because increased brain size enhances the chances of avoiding death.

A rather different explanation of the association between brain weight and longevity has recently been suggested by Sacher and Staffeldt (1974). They found that there is a strong correlation between gestation time and brain weight at birth. Mammals with large brains have long gestation times. Sacher and Staffeldt believe that in order for large brains to develop, gestation times have to be long and litter sizes small. If this is so, selection for increased brain size would result in a decreased reproductive rate. A consequence of this might be that natural selection would favour an increased life-span, because this would allow a longer reproductive period to compensate for the decreased reproductive rate. Thus, according to this argument, the long life-spans of large-brained mammals could be the secondary consequences of selection for increased brain size.

4.2 The life-span of non-mammalian vertebrates

Some of the maximum-longevity records for non-mammalian vertebrates are given in Table 4.2. The table is based on data given by Comfort (1964) who gives the source of each record. As with so many of the mammalian longevity records, the life-spans given are unlikely to be very reliable, because so few animals have been kept in captivity.

The data for birds come mainly from zoo records; as we discussed in the previous chapter, it is very unlikely that many birds in the wild reach anything like their maximum potential longevity. In captivity, the life-spans of even the smaller birds seem to be long compared with those of mammals. Comfort cites a case of a chaffinch living for 29 years in captivity, far longer than any mammal of a comparable size. Life-table data for birds in captivity are sparse, but in one study of the longevity of a group of 39 Bengalese finches the age at death of the oldest survivor was nearly ten years. It would be interesting to know whether the relation between the longevity, brain and body weights of birds is similar to that found by Sacher for mammals. From the data available it appears that there is only a slight tendency for the larger birds to have longer life-spans than the smaller species.

Reptiles are noted for their long life. There are several well-authenticated records of tortoises living for more than 100 years. According to Comfort, it

Table 4.2 Maximum recorded life-spans for non-mammalian vertebrates (based on data given by Comfort, 1964).

Species	Common name	Maximum life-span (years)
Birds		
Bubo bubo	eagle owl	68
Coracopsis vasa	vasa parrot	54
Pelicanus onocrotalus	white pelican	51
Aquila chrysaëtos	golden eagle	46
Megalornis grus	grey crane	43
Larus argentatus	herring gull	41
Sarcorhamphus papa	king vulture	40
Anser anser domesticus	domestic goose	35
Columba livia domestica	domestic pigeon	30
Struthio camelus	ostrich	27
Goura cristata	crowned pigeon	16
Reptiles		
Testudo sumeiri	Marion's tortoise	152+
Testudo marginata	margined tortoise	28
Terrapene carolina	Carolina box-tortoise	123+
Clemmys guttata	speckled terrapin	42+
Caretta caretta	loggerhead turtle	33
Alligator sinensis	Chinese alligator	52
Eunectes murinus	anaconda snake	29
Anguis fragilis	slow-worm lizard	33
Sphenodon punctatus	tuatara	28+
Amphibians		
Megalobatrachus japonicus	giant salamander	52+
Salamandra salamandra	European common salamander	24
Bufo bufo	common toad	36
Xenopus laevis	African clawed toad	15
Rana temporaria	European common frog	12+
Triturus pyrrhogaster	Japanese newt	25

is likely that many of the other reptiles are potentially long-lived although, because animals such as snakes are difficult to keep in zoos, the longevity records do not appear to be great. Data for amphibia are very limited but, in spite of the paucity of information, the maximum recorded life-spans of some of the smaller species are quite long.

There is rather more speculation about the longevity and senescence of fish than there is factual knowledge. Facts are of interest and importance, because it has been suggested that, unlike terrestrial vertebrates, fish show no senescence and never die a "natural" death. This conclusion was reached by Bidder more than 50 years ago. He believed that many fish were capable of continued growth throughout life, and that their lack of senescence was associated with their indeterminate growth. According to Bidder, since life on land sets a mechanical limit to size, the transition from an aquatic to a terrestrial environment involved the evolution in early land vertebrates of a size-regulator mechanism. This regulator mechanism produces a steady decrease in growth with age until the optimum adult size is reached, and Bidder suggested "that senescence is the result of the continued action of the regulator after growth has stopped". Thus, according to this hypothesis, senescence is the by-product of the evolution of determinate size.

If Bidder's ideas are correct, then there are two types of vertebrate, one of which has a determinate size and shows senescence, and the other type which shows no senescence and has an indeterminate size. Unfortunately information about both ageing and the growth rates of mature fish is not extensive. It is certainly true that many of the large teleosts continue to grow for very long periods of time, although the rate of growth tends to decrease with age. The sturgeon continues to grow for at least 30 years. It is also true that some fish do live for a very long time. Reliable reports suggest that ages of over 70 years are not uncommon for the sturgeon in natural conditions. Goldfish commonly live 17 years and have been reported to live for as long as 30–40 years in aquarium conditions. It is possible to obtain life-table data for natural populations of fish since an individual's age can often be assessed by counting the annual growth rings in otiliths, scales, opercular bones or fin rays. However, most of the populations which have been studied are for fish of economic importance and, since fishing affects survival chances in a non-random way, the data obtained are often difficult to interpret. The studies which have been made show that natural mortality in populations of large fish is very high, and the survival curves which are obtained are often of the exponential die-away type. Although this type of curve is characteristic of populations of animals which do not show senescence, it is also found with animals such as wild birds, in which the death rate is so high that few animals live long enough for an increase in the force of mortality to become apparent. Life-table data from wild populations cannot, therefore, be taken as evidence that senescence does not occur in a particular species of fish.

Some fish life-tables do show a slight increase in the force of mortality with age (Gerking, 1957). This is true for life-tables for the sturgeon, some herring and whitefish populations. A much more sudden and dramatic increase in the force of mortality is found for those species (such as the Pacific salmon) where nearly all individuals die after spawning for the first time. Natural populations of fish therefore show a range of types of survival curve, from those which are very rectangular to those which are characteristic of animals with indeterminate life-spans. Thus there is in fact little evidence from life-table data to support the conclusion that absence of senescence is a characteristic of fish, although of course the possibility that some do not undergo an age-related deterioration cannot be ruled out. Studies of physiological performance in fish of different ages and sizes would be valuable; at present, apart from evidence that some fish show a decline in reproductive capacity with age, little physiological information is available.

The most detailed investigation of the relation between growth and ageing of fish in aquarium conditions was made by Comfort (1964) who used the guppy *Lebistes reticulatus*. In this species the maximum longevity is about 5 years; the male grows to a limited size, but the female shows indeterminate growth. Comfort was able to control growth by manipulating the amount of food and space available to the fish. He found that, in all of the conditions which he used, he obtained life-tables which showed the pattern typical of senescence – the force of mortality increased with age. Contrary to what would be expected from Bidder's hypothesis, senescence did take place while the guppies were still capable of growth. Since the growth characteristics of some species of fish living in natural conditions are known, Comfort was able to calculate the maximum longevity expected for some of them on the basis of the relation between growth and longevity that he found in the guppy. Assuming that growth and survival in the stickleback, cod, hake and plaice are related in the same way as in the guppy, their growth characteristics lead to expected longevities of up to 5, 20, 40 and 60 years respectively. These values exceed those recorded for wild fish of these species. Therefore, if Comfort's extrapolation from the guppy to these fish is valid, it does suggest that evidence of senescence in natural populations should not be expected unless large amounts of reliable life-table data are available, because so few fish achieve anything like their maximum longevity potential.

We shall return to the subject of the relation between the rate of growth and ageing in the next chapter, since there is evidence from fish and other animals that longevity and senescence are in some way related to the rate of growth and development. However, although the evidence is far from conclusive, it seems unlikely that growth and ageing are related in the way that Bidder suggested, because there is little reason to believe that fish show no senescence, even if they do have indeterminate growth.

4.3   The life-span of invertebrates

Comfort (1964) has collected together longevity records for more than 250
different species of invertebrates from different phyla and classes. Table 4.3
gives some of these records; usually the longest life-span listed for each class
or phylum has been chosen. The records for the different species are not
really comparable because some are based on laboratory life-tables, some
on observations of single individuals in captivity, some on direct observations of animals in their natural environment, and some on age estimates
from growth rings. Furthermore, it is well established that environmental
factors such as temperature can have very marked effects on the longevity
of invertebrates, so at best the longevity records given can provide only a
very approximate idea of relative life-spans. It must also be borne in mind
that the "life-span" often means different things for different species. For example, for many insects the life-span given is the survival time of the imago,
yet frequently the length of the pre-imaginal stages is much greater than this,
particularly for the species with non-feeding imagoes. It is also difficult to
decide on the life-span of animals such as some of the planarians which can
divide by fission to form new individuals.

It is impossible to survey in detail in this chapter the whole range of invertebrate life-cycles and life-spans. Comfort's book summarizes and
evaluates much of the available data, so our discussion here will be limited
to a brief consideration of the important question:

Is there any evidence that some of the invertebrates do not show senescence?

Comfort concluded that the strongest evidence for indeterminate life-spans
came from data for the coelenterates. There are well-substantiated records
of sea anemones living for more than 80-90 years. This very long life-span
may be associated with the well-known ability of coelenterates to renew or
replace worn-out or damaged parts. Even if the extreme longevity of some
actinians does reflect the absence of senescence in some species in this class,
indeterminate life-spans are certainly not found in all coelenterates. For example, for some of the colonial hydroids, it is known that the life-spans of
individual hydranths are limited.

The other phylum for which Comfort believes that "the indeterminacy of
life-span cannot be excluded" is the Mollusca. Some of the smaller molluscs
are known to have relatively short determinate life-spans: laboratory-kept
populations of the pulmonate *Limnaea columella* show a typical rectangular
type of survival curve with a maximum longevity of about 7 months.
Natural populations of the bivalves *Nucula turgida* and *Amphidesma ven-*

E

tricosum have also been found to show an increased force of mortality with age, indicating that they too undergo senescent changes. In other species there is no evidence of senescence. Possibly the longest-lived invertebrate

Table 4.3 Maximum recorded longevities for some invertebrates (based on data taken from Comfort, 1964).

Phylum and Class	Species	Maximum life-span	Evi-dence
Porifera			
Demospongiae	*Suberites carnosus*	15 y	c
Coelenterata			
Anthozoa	*Cereus pedunculatus*	85–90 y	c
Platyhelminthes			
Cestoda	*Taeniarhynchus saginatus*	>35 y	h
Turbellaria	*Dugesia tigrina*	6–7 y	c
Aschelminthes			
Nematoda	*Wucheria bancrofti*	17 y	h
Rotifera	*Callidina* sp.	5 mo	c
Annelida			
Polychaeta	*Sabella pavonina*	>10 y	c
Oligochaeta	*Lumbricus terrestris*	5–6 y	c
Arthropoda			
Arachnida	*Filistata insidiatrix*	11 y	c
Crustacea			
S. C. Cirripedia	*Balanus balanoides*	>5 y	w
S. C. Malacostraca	*Astacus*	15–25 y	?
Insecta			
O. Ephemeroptera	*Cloëon dipterum*	4 w	c
O. Isoptera	*Neotermes castaneus*	>25 y	w
O. Lepidoptera	*Maniola jurtina*	44 d	c
O. Coleoptera	*Blaps gigas*	>10 y	c
O. Hymenoptera	*Lasius niger*	>19 y	c
Echinodermata			
Echinoidea	*Echinus esculentus*	>8 y	w
Asteroidea	*Marthasterias glacialis*	>7 y	c
Mollusca			
Amphineura	*Chiton tuberculatus*	12 y	w
Gastropoda			
S. C. Prosobranchia	*Patella vulgata*	15 y	wg
S. C. Opisthobranchia	*Haminea hydatis*	4 y	w
S. C. Pulmonata	*Rumina decollata*	12 y	c
Bivalvia	*Margaritana margaritifera*	70–80 y	wg
Cephalopoda	*Loligo pealii*	3–4 y	w

Abbreviations

Age: y = years, mo = months, w = weeks, d = days.

Evidence: c = kept in captivity, w = in wild conditions, g = age estimate based on growth, h = host case history.

known is the fresh-water mussel *Margaritana margaritifera* which, on the basis of shell growth rings, has been estimated to live for up to 100 years.

In theory, the shell structure of many molluscs enables estimates to be made of not only age, but also growth rates, so it might be thought that molluscs would be excellent material for investigating the relation between growth and ageing. However, the difficulty is that, in the absence of growth, the annual growth rings are not formed. Thus there is no adequate way of knowing if and when periods of arrested growth have occurred. The studies of growth and ageing which have been made suggest that in many species growth continues up to the maximum recorded age. In fact, the position with regard to growth and senescence in molluscs seems to be very similar to that for fish: some species undoubtedly show senescence, but for others there is no reason to believe that it does occur, although the data are not really sufficient to justify the belief that they have indeterminate life-spans. Similarly, although growth is known to be limited in some species, in others it does appear to continue throughout life. As with the fish, more information might provide valuable insights into the relation between growth and longevity.

4.4 The life-span of protozoan clones

The early literature about gerontology contains many papers dealing with the problem of whether or not protozoan cultures are immortal. It was generally believed that they were, but there were repeated reports of cultures which died out after a few months. It was realized that, as with so many other animals, failure to survive might indicate simply that inappropriate environmental conditions had been provided, rather than that senescent changes had occurred. Consequently, for many years the arguments continued with some people claiming that Protozoa were immortal, and others suggesting that they showed clonal senescence. The problem is still far from resolved, but for a few species experimental work has shown fairly clearly how in certain conditions some protozoan clones do undergo senescence, while in other conditions they do not.

Much of the experimental work has been concentrated on the ciliates, particularly *Paramecium aurelia*. It is now certain that *Paramecium* and several other ciliates show clonal ageing (Siegel, 1967). In order to understand the nature of the ageing process shown by these ciliates, it is necessary to give a brief and rather crude outline of their methods of reproduction. *P. aurelia* will be used as an example. The ciliates have two types of nuclei: large polyploid macronuclei which control the general metabolism of the cells, and small diploid micronuclei which are important in sexual reproduction. The macronuclei can be thought of as controlling the somatic functions of the cell, the micronuclei as controlling the germinal functions. *P. aurelia* has one macronucleus and two micronuclei. It can produce asexually by binary fission: each micronucleus divides mitotically to produce identical daughter nuclei, and the macronucleus also divides so that each daughter cell has two micronuclei and a macronucleus. In addition to simple fission, two types of sexual process are known for *P. aurelia*: conjugation which involves mating between individuals of complementary mating types, and autogamy which is a form of self-fertilization. During conjugation, the two micronuclei in each individual of a pair of mates divide meiotically so that 8 haploid nuclei are formed in each cell. Seven of these nuclei disintegrate, and the remaining one divides mitotically to produce 2 gamete nuclei in each cell. Reciprocal exchange of one of the gamete nuclei occurs between the two conjugating cells. The gamete nuclei then fuse, and the two conjugating cells separate. The new diploid nucleus undergoes two mitotic divisions to produce two new micronuclei and two new macronuclei; the original macronucleus has by this time disintegrated. At the next cell division each micronucleus divides mitotically, and one macronucleus passes to each daughter cell, thus restoring the original complement of two micronuclei and one macronucleus per cell. The most important things to remember about this complex mating process are that it involves the exchange of genetic material between cells and the formation of á new macronucleus. Autogamy, the other type of sexual process, is very similar to conjugation in many ways, but no genetic material is exchanged between cells. The whole sexual process occurs within a single cell. The types of nuclear divisions which occur are the same as those in conjugation, but instead of exchanging gamete nuclei with another cell, the two identical sister gamete nuclei within each cell fuse to form a new diploid nucleus. The processes by which this nucleus then divides to produce new micro- and macronuclei are exactly the same as those following the formation of the new diploid nucleus in conjugation. The old macronucleus is replaced by a new one.

Autogamy and conjugation do not normally occur in culture conditions which allow high asexual fission rates. If a clone has been initiated with a cell which has just been produced by autogamy or conjugation, it is usually capable of many generations of asexual reproduction – up to 350 fissions in some strains of *P. aurelia*. However, eventually, unless sexual reproduction is allowed, the fission rate declines, abnormal cells are produced, and the clone dies out. The clone does not have an indefinite life-span.

Conjugation or autogamy can be induced by semi-starvation, but clonal age affects the ability of individual cells to take part in sexual processes. During the first fissions of a newly initiated clone, the cells are incapable of conjugation or autogamy. This early period of "sexual immaturity" is followed by a period of "maturity" in which cells will conjugate if they are given the appropriate conditions, but will not go through autogamy. Following maturity there is a transition period during which cells are capable of either conjugation or autogamy, but eventually "senescence" begins and the cells can undergo autogamy but not conjugation. During senescence the viability of the progeny clones produced as a result of autogamy gradually gets less, until in extreme old age it is very difficult to start a new clone. Thus the original clone is no longer able to found new clones by sexual processes, or to continue its own line of asexual fission.

Senescent changes which are comparable, although not identical, with those found in *P. aurelia* have been found in other *Paramecium* species and also in other genera of ciliates, e.g. *Euplotes* and *Tetrahymena*. The ciliates are not therefore immortal since, unless the nuclear reorganization involved in conjugation or autogamy occurs, cultures invariably die out. The renewal of the macronucleus seems to be essential for the rejuvenation of a colony. In many ways, of course, the type of ageing and senescence shown by these ciliates is analogous to that shown by most Metazoa, where the somatic cells have only a limited life-span and the line can only be continued when sexual reproduction initiates a new individual with a new soma.

Although the clonal senescence shown by ciliates is interesting, it must be remembered that ciliates are unique in having two distinct types of nucleus. Studies of Protozoa such as *Amoeba* are possibly more relevant to understanding ageing in Metazoa since, at least superficially, they resemble metazoan somatic cells. The most commonly studied species, *A. proteus* and *A. discoides*, are believed to lack a sexual process; they divide by simple binary fission in a way which resembles the mitotic division seen in metazoan somatic cells. Do they show any evidence of senescence, or are all clones potentially immortal? Danielli and Muggleton (1959) have investigated this problem. They found that, when they kept amoebae in culture conditions which provided a rich supply of the food source, the amoebae would grow and divide repeatedly. Under these conditions of logarithmic growth, the cultures could be maintained indefinitely. There was no evidence of death of individual cells, apart from that due to accidents. Therefore the cultures kept on this "growth" diet were immortal; they had indeterminate life-spans. If, however, amoebae were kept on a less-rich diet, a "maintenance" diet, they did not divide, and eventually died. The most interesting observation was the effect of keeping the amoebae on a maintenance diet for a few weeks, and then transferring them to the growth diet. They did not, as might be expected, resume growth and multiplication and continue indefinitely. Instead it was found that, although growth and division were resumed, the cultures had only a limited life-span of between 30 days and 30 weeks. In Danielli and Muggleton's terminology, they became "spanned". Their exact life-span depended on the conditions of the maintenance diet. Two types of amoebae were present in the spanned cultures. One type was capable of normal logarithmic multiplication, with one cell dividing to give two daughter cells, each of which could divide in turn to give two daughter cells, and so on. Eventually, however, both of the daughter cells died. The other type of amoeba was also capable of repeated division, but each division resulted in one viable cell and one inviable cell until ultimately, after a number of divisions, both daughter cells died.

The reason why a short period on the maintenance diet converts an immortal culture into a culture with a limited life-span is not known, but these experimental results obtained with amoeba are worth remembering when thinking about the results obtained in *in vitro* work with metazoan cells (see chapter 7). What does seem to be clear from Danielli and Muggleton's experiments is that, even for asexual species, the mortality or immortality of protozoan cultures depends in a rather subtle way on the culture conditions.

4.5   The inheritance of longevity in man

In the previous sections we have seen how each animal species usually has its own characteristic life-span. Since what determines whether an animal belongs to one particular species or another is its genetic constitution, it must follow that genetic differences are responsible for the differences in the longevities of different species. In chapter 3 we considered how longevity and ageing might have evolved in response to natural selection. In doing so, we assumed that there were genetic differences between individuals which would affect longevity and ageing. It is now necessary to look at some of the evidence which shows that senescence and longevity are in fact affected by hereditary factors, and to assess the extent to which the differences in longevity found within a species, as well as those between species, are the result of genetic differences.

It has often been said that the best way of ensuring that one lives to an old age is to choose long-lived parents and grandparents. Is it really true that you are more likely to live a long time if your immediate ancestors did? If so, is it because you inherited some of their genes, or is there another explanation? Unfortunately the analysis of the inheritance of longevity in man is difficult. Not the least of the difficulties is the well-known effect of environmental conditions on human longevity. For example, the trend over the past century for average longevity to increase as a result of improved nutrition, public health measures and medical care must confuse the picture and complicate the interpretation of longevity data. It is always difficult in studies of the inheritance of continuously varying characters, such as height, weight or intelligence, to decide the extent to which the similarities seen in families are due to hereditary factors, and the extent to which they are due to the similarities in the environments of the individuals in a family. This difficulty is even more marked in studies of longevity. The investigator usually cannot take his own measurements of the character in question, or make his own assessment of the environment. He has to rely on people's memory of their relative's age at death, the cause of death, and the environmental conditions under which life was lived. In spite of the difficulties, however, a number of workers in the early part of this century applied to longevity data the statistical techniques which had been developed to analyse the amount of the variation between individuals which could be accounted for by genetic differences. The data which they analysed came from a variety of sources, such as insurance company records, family genealogies, and in a few cases (e.g. in Pearl's classic study) from interviews with old people, in which they were asked to recall their relatives' ages at death. Gradually a fairly consistent body of evidence was built up which showed that there was a positive correlation between the longevity of parents and offspring. Nevertheless, in spite of the consistency, the evidence from many of these early studies must be treated with some reservation, since the data on which they were based were not really adequate; genealogies were incomplete, the life-spans could not be verified by the investigator, and the samples used were non-random. In more recent studies, attempts have been made to avoid most of these pitfalls. The preliminary results of one recent study by Abbott et al. (1974) are shown in Table 4.4. Although the study is not yet complete, the results tend to confirm the existence of a relation between the age at death of the parents and the life-span of the children.

The sample studied by Abbott et al. consisted of over 9000 progeny of 1766 people who were known to have died at an age of 90 or more. The nonagenarians were some of those who had been identified by Pearl in a study of human longevity which was reported in 1943. Abbott et al. traced all the nonagenarians' descendants and then looked at the life-span of the non-proband parent and that of the offspring. The non-proband parent is the husband or wife of the nonagenarian. Although the study is not yet com-

Table 4.4 Length of life of the progeny in families in which one parent lived for more than 90 years (based on data taken from Abbott *et al*, 1974).

(i) Survivorship* of the offspring when the father lived to 90+

Sex of offspring	Mother's age at death		
	60 or less	61 – 80	81 or more
male	67.6	71.4	73.2
female	73.8	74.1	77.2
combined	70.9	72.8	75.1

(ii) Survivorship* of the offspring when the mother lived to 90+

Sex of offspring	Father's age at death		
	60 or less	61 – 80	81 or more
male	67.0	69.3	70.9
female	73.0	73.5	73.3
combined	69.8	71.4	72.1

*Each value is an estimated average based on over 295 offspring

plete, because some of the offspring are not yet dead, the large sample involved makes it probable that the estimates given in Table 4.4 are fairly accurate. The data tend to support the early workers' conclusion that long-lived parents produce long-lived children, although the mother's longevity seems to have more influence than does the father's.

If, as the evidence suggests, there is a correlation between the life-spans of parents and children, is it proof of a genetic component in longevity? The answer to this question is no, because environmental factors could be the cause of the correlation. For example, infectious diseases, such as tuberculosis which can be passed from parents to children, could influence the life-spans of both in a similar way; parents and children are more likely to share the same occupation and occupational hazards than unrelated people, and this will tend to make their life-spans more similar; parents and children are likely to have similar eating habits and, if diet affects longevity, this will mean that their longevities will tend to be closer than those of unrelated people. All of these environmental factors could contribute to the observed correlation between length of life of parents and children. Abbott *et al*. tend to favour a non-genetic explanation of the correlation that they found.

Although Abbott *et al*. suggest that their data can be explained in non-genetic terms, people who have used the twin-study method to investigate longevity have concluded that a genetic component is involved. In the twin-study method of investigating the inheritance of human characters, the differences between members of pairs of monozygotic twins are compared with the differences between members of pairs of dizygotic twins. Monozygotic or one-egg· twins develop from a single egg fertilized by a single sperm. At an early cleavage stage this fertilized egg divides into two independent embryos which, since they originate from the same zygote, are genetically identical. Dizygotic or two-egg twins are produced when two distinct eggs are each fertilized and develop in the womb at the same time. Genetically, since dizygotic twins originate from two separate eggs and two separate sperms, they are no more alike than any other brothers and sisters. The value of twins for studying the influence of genetic and environmental factors on a particular character is the result of the genetic similarity of monozygotic twins. Generally speaking, differences between the members of a pair of monozygotic twins are the result of environmental effects; on the other hand, intrapair differences in dizygotic twins are the result of both genetic and environmental factors. Therefore, if genotype influences a character, a bigger intrapair difference would be expected for dizygotic twins than for monozygotic twins. A number of workers have shown that the life-spans of monozygotic twins are more similar than those of dizygotic twins. Figure 4.4 shows the results from a survey by Kallmann and Jarvik (1959). Some of the sample sizes were rather small, and only twin pairs in

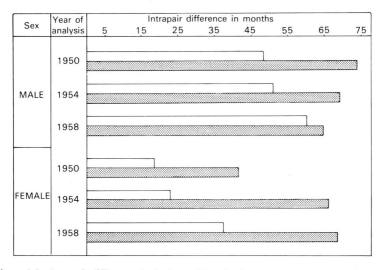

Figure 4.4 Intrapair differences in the longevities of twins. Unhatched blocks monozygotic twins, hatched blocks dizygotic twins (based on data from Kallmann and Jarvik, 1959).

which both partners died of natural causes after the age of 60 were included, but the data clearly show that the intrapair differences were smaller for monozygotic twins than for dizygotic twins. Other studies have produced similar results. For example, in a study of over 200 pairs of monozygotic and 400 pairs of dizygotic Danish twins, in which the investigator did not use a minimum age for death, the mean intrapair difference was found to be 14.5 years for monozygotic, and 18.7 for dizygotic twins.

In their twin study Kallmann and his co-workers also looked at the causes of death. They found that one-egg twins were slightly more likely to have similar causes of death than two-egg twins. Furthermore, in the senescent period, measurements of intellectual performances which are known to decline with age were more similar in one-egg than in two-egg twins.

Although these twin-studies do suggest that hereditary factors are important in determining longevity, it is well known that there may be reasons not directly related to their genetic similarity which make monozygotic twins more similar than dizygotic twins. Their physical resemblance may make parents and other people treat them as a unit rather than as two separate people, and their actions and reactions with respect to each other may be different from those of normal sibs. Furthermore, twins are a rather atypical section of the population, so it may be unwise to generalize about the hereditary component in longevity on the basis of twin studies. After a detailed review of the literature on the inheritance of longevity in man, Cohen (1964) stated:

it is concluded that at present, despite all the recorded information and presumptive evidence, the problem of the genetic aspects of mortality and life-span remains to be resolved.

Rather more conclusive evidence about the inheritance of longevity has come from studies with experimental animals but, before considering this work, mention must be made of some of the "premature ageing" syndromes which are known in man. The two most well-known types of progeria are Werner's syndrome and Hutchinson-Gilford syndrome. Hutchinson-Gilford syndrome, or infantile progeria, usually begins to show itself before the child's first birthday; growth is retarded, and the result is severe dwarfing with an abnormal physical appearance. The children usually do not mature sexually, and death occurs before the age of thirty. Very early in life, hair is lost, the skin appears to be abnormal, and severe atherosclerosis develops. In some ways, therefore, the children appear to be prematurely aged. The genetic basis of the condition is not firmly established, but there is a little evidence suggesting that it may be due to an autosomal recessive gene. For Werner's syndrome, the evidence that it is an autosomal recessive trait is fairly strong. In this type of progeria, premature ageing usually does not develop until at least late adolescence, so, although sufferers may be short, they are usually not dwarfs; sexual maturity normally occurs, although the secondary sexual characters are poorly developed. Typically, people with Werner's syndrome show many of the following characteristics: premature hair-greying and baldness, changes in skin pigmentation and texture, cataracts, osteoporosis, atherosclerosis, a tendency to diabetes, cerebral cortical atrophy, and ulcerations of the skin of the limbs. Many of these features resemble those found during normal senescence, and the mean life-span of the sufferers is only 47 years. Nevertheless, there are too many differences between senescent people and those with Werner's syndrome to be confident that precocious or accelerated ageing has occurred in the latter. For example, the type of cataract in Werner's syndrome is different from that found commonly in old people, the loss of hair is generalized in Werner's syndrome, whereas in normal ageing it is mainly on the scalp and, whereas in normal people osteoporosis usually shows itself in the spine, in people suffering from Werner's syndrome it is found mainly in the distal extremities. The number and size of these differences suggest that understanding the biochemical basis of Werner's syndrome is unlikely to lead to an understanding of the way in which normal ageing processes are controlled, but there do seem to be some similarities with normal ageing.

4.6 The inheritance of longevity in experimental animals

Theoretically the genetic basis of longevity should be much more easy to study in experimental animals than it is in man, because controlled breeding experiments can be carried out. It must be remembered, though, that longevity is a rather unusual character in that it cannot be measured accurately until the opportunity to breed from the animal has been lost! Also, even when an animal has survived for long enough for one to feel confident that it is going to be a "long-lived" individual, it may be too late to breed from it because fertility often declines to zero long before death occurs. Consequently it is rather difficult to apply many of the established techniques for studying quantitative characters to the study of longevity. Selection experiments are difficult because, at the time when crosses have to be made, the life-spans of the parents and indeed frequently of the grandparents are not known. Experimental procedures which allow for this lack of information at the time of breeding can be devised, but the number of animals which have to be used to ensure that the appropriate matings are made makes the experiments very costly if mammals are used.

There is a further complication in carrying out selection experiments, namely, the possibility that the age of the mother may influence the length of life of her offspring. A maternal-age effect has been reported for a number of different species including man, the housefly, *Drosophila*, and the mealworm *Tenebrio molitor*, although the evidence from different investigations is not always consistent. Usually the reports suggest that the offspring of older mothers have shorter life-spans, and there is no reason to think that the effect lasts for more than one generation. For some species, however, the effects of maternal age on longevity appear to be carried over into subsequent generations and are cumulative. The cumulative effect is usually referred to as a "Lansing Effect", since the first detailed investigation of the phenomenon was made by Lansing (1947). He studied parthenogenetic rotifers whose reproduction involves ameiotic division of the female germ cells, resulting in clones of genetically identical offspring. In spite of the fact that all of the offspring had the same genotype, Lansing found that those coming from eggs laid by old mothers had shorter life-spans than those from eggs laid by young mothers. The interesting observation was that a clone which was propagated in each generation by using eggs from old mothers always became extinct, because the longevity of each succeeding generation became less and less. The life-span of individuals in lines maintained through young mothers remained constant, or even increased slightly. In the "old" lines, the clones could be rejuvenated again by resuming breeding through young parents. This indicated that the effect was reversible. Lansing believed that a cytoplasmic factor was influencing longevity.

There are many scattered reports of successful and unsuccessful attempts to demonstrate a Lansing effect in other species. Although far from conclusive, the available evidence does suggest that in some animals there may be an effect of maternal age on longevity, and that this effect may extend through several generations. The cause of this phenomenon is not known, but the possible existence of a Lansing effect, as well as a simple maternal-age effect, has to be considered when studying the inheritance of longevity.

Studies made with mammals and insects have shown that there are strain-specific differences in average life-spans, and also that some mutant genes have characteristic effects on longevity. For example, many years ago Raymond Pearl showed that *D. melanogaster* homozygous for the wing mutant *vestigial* had a shorter life-span than normal wild-type flies. Since *vestigial* is a typical Mendelian recessive character, crosses between *vestigial* and wild-type flies produce an F_1 generation in which all the flies are phenotypically wild type, and an F_2 generation in which three quarters are wild type and one quarter are *vestigial*. Pearl found that the *vestigial* flies in the F_2 generation had short life-spans, similar to those of their *vestigial* grandparents, and that the wild-type flies were correspondingly long-lived. Thus the mutant had an effect on longevity as well as on wing structure. Many comparable cases of a single gene affecting longevity are known in *Drosophila* and in the mouse.

Convincing evidence of the importance of genotype in determining longevity comes from work with inbred strains of animals. Inbred strains are produced and maintained by mating together close relatives, often brothers and sisters. As a result of this method of breeding, the individuals within an inbred strain are genetically much more uniform than those in normal out-bred strains, and they are highly homozygous. Often they are also relatively short-lived, although each inbred line tends to have its own characteristic life-span. Figure 4.5 shows survival curves for two inbred strains of *D. sub-obscura* and for the F_1 hybrids from crosses between them. It can be seen that the hybrid flies have far longer life-spans than the inbred flies. The hybrids live about the same length of time as outbred flies or the laboratory-reared offspring of wild-caught flies.

Short life-spans are also usual for inbred strains of mice. In mice, too, the F_1 offspring from a cross between two inbred lines live longer than either parental strain.

We still do not understand fully the causes of "inbreeding depression" and "hybrid vigour", such as has been found in these studies of longevity.

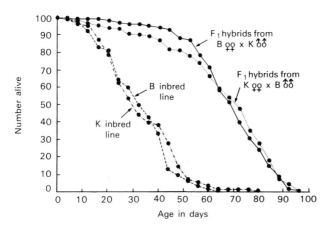

Figure 4.5 Survival curves for inbred and hybrid *Drosophila subobscura* (redrawn from Clarke and Maynard Smith, 1955).

At least part of the reason why F_1 hybrids survive longer than inbred individuals may be due to the fact that two inbred strains are likely to be homozygous for different recessive genes. If some of these genes affect longevity adversely, then, although the inbred lines have short life-spans, the F_1 generation is unlikely to be affected, because the animals will be heterozygous at most loci. For the mouse there is ample evidence to show that different inbred lines have different characteristic causes of death. For example, a particular type of neoplasia may be very common in one strain but not in another. Although this is far from being conclusive evidence, it does suggest that the different inbred lines do indeed carry different deleterious genes.

4.7 Genotype and the rate of ageing

Genotype undoubtedly affects longevity, but does it affect the rate of ageing? This is a difficult question to answer, because there has been little systematic study of the physiological and biochemical changes which accompany ageing in animals of different genotypes. It would be interesting to know whether inbred animals are born physiologically "older", or whether they show accelerated ageing changes. In terms of the model that we were using in chapter 1, do they have less vitality at birth, or is the rate of loss of vitality greater? Possibly all that is different in inbred strains is that they are more susceptible to one particular type of disease.

Some work with *Drosophila* suggests that newly emerged inbred flies are less tolerant of extreme high temperatures and are less able to acclimatize to temperature changes than hybrid flies. Their rate of egg production is also lower. They therefore resemble hybrid flies of greater age. This could be taken to indicate that inbred flies are "older" at the time of emergence than hybrid flies. However, other studies of *Drosophila* show that this is too simple an interpretation. For example, the way in which oxygen consumption changes with age is both quantitatively and qualitatively different in inbred and hybrid flies.

The relative amount of variation between individuals for some quantitative characters, such as weight and fecundity, has been shown to be greater in inbred strains than in hybrid animals. If variation between individuals which are genetically similar can be used as a measurement of their homeostatic ability, inbred strains would seem to have a lower homeostatic ability than hybrids. Since declining homeostatic ability is characteristic of ageing, young inbred flies could be thought of as biologically old. However, a very detailed study comparing many physiological and

biochemical changes in inbred and hybrid flies would be necessary to sub-
stantiate this, and to understand fully the basis of the differences in their
life-spans.

4.8 Sex and longevity

A number of people have stated that in most species the female sex outlives
the male. This is certainly true in man where, in both developed and underdeveloped countries, the average and maximum life-spans are greater for
women. What is the reason for this difference? Although many suggestions
have been made, no really satisfactory explanation seems to have been
produced. It is tempting to associate the difference with the different
chromosomal constitutions of men and women. Women have two X
chromosomes, men a single X and a Y; men therefore carry only one copy
of X-linked genes, women carry two. If longevity differences are due to
different dosages of X-linked genes, it should be true for most species that
the females live longer than the males, since in most groups of animals the
female is the homogametic sex. However, in spite of statements to the contrary, it is not clear that this is the general rule. In the mouse and in
Drosophila, the strain determines to a large extent which sex has the greater
life-span; it is certainly not true that females always live longer than males.
In the birds, the male is the homogametic sex, yet the available data suggest
that the female usually has the greater life-span. There is therefore little
reason to believe that sex differences in longevity are correlated with
different dosages of X-linked genes.

In some animals the relative longevities of the sexes have been shown to
depend on sexual activity. In *Drosophila*, virgin females generally live longer
than mated females, and there are some reports that this is also true for
males. For females, the shorter life-span of mated flies is known to be
associated with their high rate of egg-production. A mated female which is
semi-sterilized by a heat shock, a chemosterilant, or a low dose of ionizing
radiation, will live as long as or longer than a virgin female kept in the same
conditions. The size of the difference between the life-spans of virgin and
mated females depends on the environmental conditions in which they are
kept.

In mice, too, virgin females usually live longer than mated females, but it
is not clear whether this difference between virgin and mated animals is
widespread in the animal kingdom. Marital status certainly affects longevity
in human populations, but not in the way which would be expected from the
data for experimental animals. The unmarried usually have shorter

life-spans than the married. However, since widowed and divorced people have average life-spans which are shorter than those of unmarried people, it seems likely that these differences are associated with social and environmental factors rather than with strictly biological differences.

CHAPTER FIVE

MODIFYING THE RATE OF AGEING AND THE LENGTH OF LIFE

IN THE LAST CHAPTER WE CONSIDERED HOW INTRINSIC CONSTITUTIONAL factors affect the length of life of individuals. In this chapter we shall be concerned with the effect of extrinsic environmental factors. No attempt will be made to give a fully comprehensive account of all of the agents which are known to affect the length of life – there are far too many of them. Instead we will concentrate on some of the experimental work which has led to, or resulted from, hypotheses about the nature of ageing processes.

Before discussing this experimental work it is necessary to emphasize again the difficulty of deducing anything about the rate of ageing from the length of life. It is very tempting to assume that if a species lives 100 days in one set of conditions and 10 days in another, ageing is more rapid in the latter conditions. Figure 5.1 is an attempt to show why this might be an incorrect assumption. The figure is based on the same kind of simple model as was used in chapter 1. The upper diagram (A) shows ageing as a loss of vitality with time, death occurring when the level of vitality falls below a threshold; the lower diagrams (B–E) show some of the different ways in which a stress or change of environment could affect the rate of ageing or length of life. In diagrams B–E, at the age indicated by the arrow, the environmental conditions are changed or a stress is applied which results in a reduction in the length of life. The reason why the life-span is reduced is different in each case.

Diagram B shows *accelerated* ageing; the rate of loss of vitality is increased. Generally speaking, the rate at which age-dependent structural, physiological and biochemical changes occur would be expected to increase if ageing is simply accelerated.

Diagram C shows what is sometimes called *precocious* ageing. Immediately after the stress is applied the animal rapidly loses vitality; it ages rapidly but, after this, ageing processes proceed at the same rate as they did prior to the application of the stress.

Diagram D illustrates the *threshold* explanation of changes in longevity.

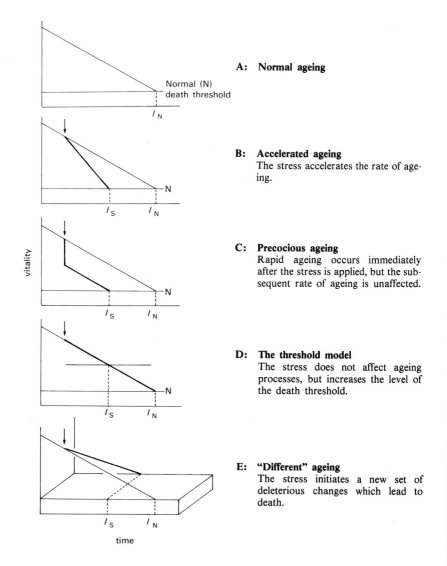

A: **Normal ageing**

B: **Accelerated ageing**
    The stress accelerates the rate of age-ing.

C: **Precocious ageing**
    Rapid ageing occurs immediately after the stress is applied, but the sub-sequent rate of ageing is unaffected.

D: **The threshold model**
    The stress does not affect ageing processes, but increases the level of the death threshold.

E: **"Different" ageing**
    The stress initiates a new set of deleterious changes which lead to death.

Figure 5.1 The rate of ageing and the life-span.
A shows normal ageing with death occurring at time l_N.
B to E show the effect of applying a stress or changing the environment at the time indicated by the arrow; death then occurs at time l_S.

There is no change in the level of vitality when the stress is applied or the environmental conditions are changed. There is also no change in the rate at which ageing processes occur. The time and rate of appearance of age-related changes are completely unaffected. What changes is the threshold level at which death occurs. The animal needs a higher level of vitality to withstand the new conditions than it did originally.

Diagram E is an example which illustrates the inadequacy of the simple model. It is an attempt to show the situation in which a stress or environmental change initiates a set of deleterious changes which are rather different from those which were causing the original age-related deterioration. In order to show this, it has been necessary to add another dimension to the picture. In adding this extra dimension we are showing what is almost certainly true, namely, that ageing is not a single simple process with a single pathway. The nature of the "loss of vitality" may be different for different individuals, and will result in death from different causes. In some animals the deterioration in one particular system may be the pacemaker for ageing changes, while in other animals it may be another system. The complex inter-relations and interactions between different systems in the body mean that many of the outward signs of ageing may often be similar in different individuals, even though the basic causes of the age-related functional decline may not be the same. Figure 5.1E is intended to show how a new stress or a change in the environment could affect life-span by changing the cause and the course of ageing processes. If longevity is changed in this way, then there is no reason why all of the age-related structural, physiological and biochemical changes which occur in the treated animals should be exactly the same as those which would have occurred without treatment. The main causes of death may well be different too.

The diagrams in figure 5.1 are much too simple to be adequate illustrations of ageing, but they do serve to show how difficult it is to decide on the basis of longevity studies alone whether or not ageing processes are affected by a particular environmental agent. Many of the experiments which have been designed to develop and test theories about the nature and causes of ageing have involved observation only of the way in which longevity is modified by stresses or environmental factors. Far less is known about the effects of these factors on age-related physiological and biochemical changes, although this information would be of great help in understanding the reasons for the change in life-span.

5.1   The rate of living and the rate of ageing in poikilotherms

The first group of inter-related ideas about the nature and causes of ageing processes which we shall consider are those which relate the rate of ageing to the rate of development and the rate of living. The idea that a high rate of living shortens the life-span has a certain puritanical attraction! To a limited extent the idea is probably correct, because a person who is very active probably "lives dangerously" and exposes himself to more risks than one who leads a less active life. He is more likely to die young, but of course this does not mean that he ages more rapidly. Similarly, although some studies have shown that manual workers tend to have shorter life-spans than other occupational groups, this need not be associated directly with the physical nature of their work, because manual workers also differ from other groups in diet and general living standards. Observations and experiments on laboratory animals provide a better way of assessing the effect of the rate of living on longevity than do studies of human actuarial statistics.

In the last chapter we considered the way in which the basal metabolic rate and longevity of different species of mammals are inter-related. Mammalian species with high metabolic rates have short life-spans. With poikilotherms it is possible to investigate the relation between metabolic rate and longevity *within* a species, because it is relatively easy to modify the metabolic rate.

When a poikilotherm such as *Drosophila* is kept at a high temperature, it normally has a higher metabolic rate and shorter life-span than it has at a low temperature. This observation is the basis of a theory which was developed by Loeb and Northrop, and later elaborated by Pearl in the early years of this century. The theory is usually called the *rate-of-living theory* and it still continues to stimulate experimentation and discussion. Loeb and Northrop found that the temperature coefficient for the rate of ageing in *Drosophila* was comparable with that of a biochemical process, i.e. the Q_{10} was about 2.5. It was assumed that the rate of ageing was inversely proportional to the life-span. They interpreted the observed temperature coefficient as an indication either that ageing was due to the loss of something which was necessary to maintain life, or that it was due to the accumulation of undesirable by-products of biochemical reactions. According to Pearl, high temperatures increased the rate of living, and a high rate of living shortened the life-span because "vitality" was used up more quickly. In other words, these early investigators believed that the effect of high temperatures was to accelerate ageing in the way shown in figure 5.1B because it accelerated metabolic rate.

Unfortunately, while it is undoubtedly true that poikilotherms have shorter life-spans at high temperatures, it is not generally agreed that this is due to ageing processes being accelerated. Clarke and Maynard Smith (1961) have suggested that the rate of ageing is independent of temperature. They believe that high temperatures shorten the life-span, not because the rate of ageing is increased, but rather because the level of vitality necessary to maintain life is higher. The *threshold theory* illustrated in figure 5.1D resulted from their interpretation of temperature experiments with *D. subobscura*. These experiments involved transferring flies which had spent the early part of their imaginal life-spans at 20°C, to 26°C. When they did this they found that, provided the transfer to the high temperature was not made too late in the life-span, the flies lived the same length of time as those which had been kept at the high temperature throughout their imaginal lives. If ageing processes are temperature-dependent, the flies should have lived longer than those kept permanently at 26°C. Similarly, they found that flies which were transferred to 20°C after a period at 26°C had the same life-span as those kept at 20°C throughout their lives. The rate-of-living hypothesis predicts that they should have had life-spans intermediate between those of flies kept permanently at 26°C and those kept permanently at 20°C.

Since flies which were transferred to 26°C at an age greater than their expectation of life at that temperature did not die immediately, Clarke and Maynard Smith proposed that the temperature-independent "ageing phase" was followed by a "dying phase" which began once vitality had fallen below the critical level necessary to maintain life at a particular temperature. They found that the length of the dying phase was temperature-dependent. Thus, according to these workers, there are two phases in ageing: a temperature-independent ageing phase followed by a temperature-dependent dying phase.

In the years since Clarke and Maynard Smith carried out their experiments, attempts have been made to repeat them using the same and other poikilotherms. Some workers claim to have confirmed their observations, others have obtained results similar to those predicted by the rate-of-living hypothesis. Therefore, at present, all that we can conclude from the mass of contradictory experimental evidence is that the effect of temperature on ageing processes in invertebrates remains to be clarified.

A rather surprising effect of temperature on longevity has been found by Liu and Walford (1975) in fish. They studied the life-span of the annual fish *Cynolebias bellottii* at 20° and 15°C. As might be expected, the life-span at 15°C was greater than the life-span at 20°C. Moreover, they found that the collagen of fish kept at the lower temperature was "younger" than that of fish of a corresponding age which had been kept at 20°C (see chapter 6). This suggests that low temperatures may indeed decrease the rate of ageing, and leads us to expect that fish transferred from one temperature to another should have life-spans of intermediate duration. However, in Liu and Walford's experiments they did not. As Table 5.1 shows, fish transferred from 20°C to 15°C when they were 8 months old lived longer than those kept continuously at 15°C. Liu and Walford interpret this observation in terms of the effect of temperature on the immune system. They believe that lowering the temperature in the latter half of life retards ageing processes because it suppresses the autoimmune responses. We shall consider the autoimmune hypothesis of ageing in the next chapter. Liu and Walford do not accept that the temperature effects which they observed had anything to do with differences in metabolic rates since the fish kept at 15°C were very active and grew more rapidly than those kept at 20°C.

Table 5.1 Temperature effects on the life-span of *Cynolebias bellottii* (Liu and Walford, 1975).

Temperature	Number of fish	Life-span (months) Mean ± standard deviation	Maximum
Continuously at 20°C	25	14.0 ± 3.9	21
15°C for 8 months, 20°C thereafter	54	15.2 ± 4.4	26
Continuously at 15°C	52	18.9 ± 5.5	32
20°C for 8 months, 15°C thereafter	14	23.5 ± 9.1	38

One interesting set of results which does support the idea that the longevity of poikilotherms depends on their rate of living is illustrated in figure 5.2. The animals used were *shaker* mutants of *D. melanogaster*. The *shaker* genes are sex-linked and semi-dominant. They affect the neurological system. Flies which carry the genes are very sensitive to environmental stimuli and are abnormally active. It was found that their metabolic rate as measured by oxygen consumption was higher than that of normal flies, and that there was a positive correlation between oxygen consumption and activity for the different mutants. The figure shows that the length of life of these mutant strains was inversely proportional to their metabolic rate. Thus these results support the hypothesis that longevity depends on the rate of living.

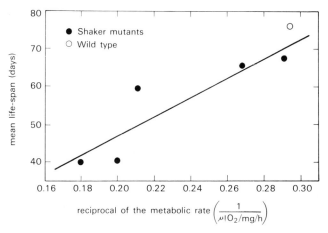

Figure 5.2   The relation between longevity and metabolic rate for shaker mutants of *Drosophila melanogaster* (redrawn from Trout and Kaplan, 1970).

5.2   Growth, nutrition and ageing

The relation between growth and senescence has already been considered briefly in chapter 4. It was concluded that there was a lack of sound evidence to support the hypothesis that animals with indeterminate growth showed no senescence. In this section we shall be more concerned with the problem of whether or not the *rate* at which animals grow affects their life-span.

One way of slowing down growth is to restrict the supply of food available to an animal. If food is restricted, then the total life-span of many different invertebrates, e.g. *Daphnia*, planarians, and some rotifers, is increased. The life-span of mammals can also be prolonged by restricting food intake. This was clearly demonstrated in some now classic experiments carried out by McCay and his colleagues more than 40 years ago (see McCay, 1952). They kept young rats on a diet which was nutritionally adequate but deficient in calories. The effect of this was to prevent the rats from reaching maturity. They remained small and immature, and could be kept in this condition for over a thousand days – far longer than the normal life-span of the strain being used. When the rats were given a normal diet again, growth was resumed, the rats matured, and eventually they died at an age much greater than of animals fed *ad libitum*. The increased life-span was a result of the prolongation of the juvenile period rather than of the adult period. McCay noted that the retarded rats had a lower incidence of diseases of the lung, middle ear and kidneys.

McCay's experiments have been repeated and extended by a number of people. In general, the results confirm the finding that dietary restriction, either in the juvenile period or throughout life, increases the total life-span. Moreover, some of the studies have shown that the time of appearance of age-associated lesions is delayed in restricted rats. For example, figure 5.3 shows some of the results of one such study in which rats were restricted from the time of weaning by 46%, i.e. they were allowed to eat only 54% of the food that they would have taken had they been allowed to eat *ad lib*. These restricted rats were smaller than the control animals, lived longer, and as the figure shows, the age of onset of diseases was later.

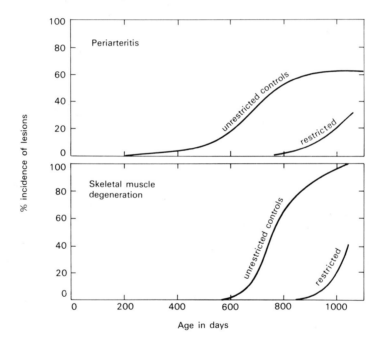

Figure 5.3   Incidence of periarteritis and skeletal muscle degeneration in rats on a restricted diet compared with those fed *ad libitum* (redrawn from Simms and Berg, 1962).

Do these studies of the effect of diet on longevity tell us anything about the relation between growth and ageing? Many gerontologists believe that ageing is genetically programmed. That is, they believe that it is essentially a continuation of development during which different parts of the genome switch on and off in an evolutionarily determined sequence. It can be argued that by stretching the developmental programme, the "clock" which governs the rate at which the ageing programme runs is also slowed down. Dietary restriction in the juvenile stage might slow ageing processes because it sets the clock to "slow". Slow growth produces slow ageing.

Unfortunately in a number of the studies of the effect of nutrition on longevity there are puzzling features which do not fit in with the simple idea that prolonging the period of growth also prolongs the period of maturity and senescence. For example, in McCay's study (and in those of other people) the total life-span did not seem to depend on the length of the period of restriction or on the ultimate size of the animals. Furthermore, Barrows and Roeder (1963) found that, although the activities of various enzymes in the livers and kidneys of restricted rats were different from those of normal rats, they were not similar to those of fully fed rats of a younger age. Therefore, at least some of the biochemical changes which are known to occur in normal ageing do not seem to be slowed down by dietary restriction. Miller and Payne (1968) found that with their rats the longest life-span was obtained by feeding the rats with a diet which supported maximum growth rate for the first 120 days, followed by a diet which was just sufficient to maintain weight thereafter. The rats were prevented from achieving their maximum weight and therefore from becoming obese. It may be that some of the restricted diets used by other workers were effective in prolonging life because they prevented or delayed the deleterious effects of obesity rather than because they affected ageing processes.

The dietary restriction experiments are interesting and important because dietary restriction is one of the very few methods of prolonging the life-span of experimental animals. Regrettably the experiments still do not provide any conclusive evidence for or against the idea that there is a relation between the rate of growth and the rate of ageing. Work in which growth hormones have been used to attempt to modify life-span and ageing has produced equally ambiguous conclusions. In the male rat, growth stops in middle age, and towards the end of the life-span there is a loss in weight. Everitt attempted to prolong the period of growth by injecting middle-aged rats with daily doses of pituitary growth hormone. He found that, although with a high dose he could increase the body weight of the rats, the treatment had no effect on longevity, and the normal decrease in weight at the end of the life-span still occurred. In experiments where the pituitary was removed, the effect on rats was similar to that of food restriction: growth stopped and the animals did not mature. However, the life-spans of the hypophysectomized rats were much shorter than those of the control animals, not longer as would be expected if slow growth caused slow ageing. Everitt did find that the hypophysectomized animals had a delayed onset of chronic nephrosis relative to the controls, and also that collagen fibres did not age as quickly as in the controls (see chapter 6). In these respects, therefore, ageing changes seemed to have been retarded, although the life-span was shorter. As a result of these and other studies, Everitt (1973) concluded that pituitary hormones are very important in controlling ageing in mammals.

Bellamy (1968) investigated the effect on mice of prednisolone, a synthetic cortisol derivative related to the adrenocorticosteroids. The growth of mice from an inbred strain was retarded by 25% by prednisolone, although there was no evidence of a difference in their food and water intake, or of a difference in the time at which sexual maturity was reached. The life-span of the treated animals was increased from one year to about 2 years, and some age-dependent physiological and biochemical changes were delayed. It seemed, therefore, that this growth inhibitor also delayed senescence. Unfortunately when Forbes (1975) repeated this experiment, using a longer-living strain of mice, he found that prednisolone had no effect on longevity. It is therefore rather difficult at present to draw any firm conclusions about the relation between growth and senescence from work with steroid hormones and related substances.

Some of the most impressive support for the idea that there is a relation between growth and longevity has come from results obtained by Lints and Lints (1971) with the fruit fly *D. melanogaster*. Growth in this insect is restricted almost entirely to the pre-imaginal stages. Lints and Lints were able to vary the length of the growth stages in two ways. The first was by rearing the larvae under different degrees of crowding. In crowded conditions the development period is extended, and the adults produced are small in size. The second method used was to rear the larvae at different temperatures. Low temperatures increase development time and also increase adult size. Notice that these two methods of increasing development time have opposite effects on adult size: low temperature increases it, high larval density decreases it. Lints and Lints looked at the length of life of the imagoes relative to both size and the length of the development period. Size and longevity were negatively correlated when larval density was varied, but positively correlated when developmental temperature was varied. Longevity did not therefore depend on size *per se*. On the other hand, imaginal longevity was positively correlated with the length of development in both the temperature and density experiments. However, the best correlation of all was obtained by considering both size and duration of development

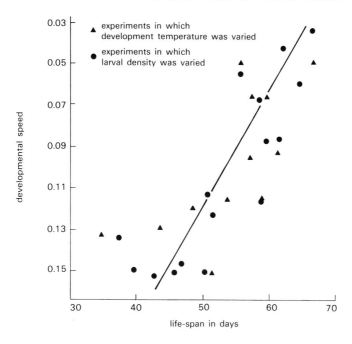

Figure 5.4 The relation between developmental speed and life-span in *Drosophila melanogaster* (redrawn from Lints and Lints, 1971).

together. This is shown in figure 5.4 where longevity is plotted against rate of development as measured by thorax size in mm^3 divided by duration of development in days. There is clearly a very good correlation between developmental speed and imaginal longevity. Slow rates of development are associated with long life-spans.

What conclusions about ageing processes can be drawn from studies of the relation between development and longevity? It may prove useful to summarize briefly the evidence that we have considered in this and earlier chapters. Firstly, Sacher's work with mammals suggests that long gestation times are associated with long life-spans, because both are correlated with the index of cephalization. Secondly, although the evidence is certainly not very good, it may be that some animals which show indeterminate growth also have indeterminate life-spans. Thirdly, the life-spans of some animals (including mammals) can be increased by dietary restriction during youth, although it is not clear how this is brought about. Fourthly, the longevity of *D. melanogaster* is negatively correlated with the speed of development.

This is a rather heterogeneous collection of data, and it is perhaps unwise to attempt to draw any general conclusions from it. Nevertheless, it does suggest that there is some kind of relation between growth and senescence. It seems to point to the idea that the slower the rate of growth and the attainment of maturity and final size, the longer the life-span. Could it be that slow development enables a "better" animal to be built because there is more opportunity for repair and replacement of defective parts? Could it be that there is a continuous development-senescence programme and, if it is set to a slow speed during development, the ageing and senescence part of the programme also runs more slowly? The available data are not really sufficiently substantial to warrant this type of speculation, but they do at least suggest that it is quite wrong to think of development and senescence as two distinct processes.

5.3   Radiation-induced life-shortening and the somatic mutation hypothesis

In the early 1960s, the theory of ageing which probably provoked more experimental work than any other was the *somatic mutation theory*. One of its main attractions was its universality – it suggested that there was a common fundamental cause of ageing in all species, even though the manifestations of senescence were very different. There are several different versions of the theory, but the basic idea is a very simple one. It is that ageing is due to the accumulation of mutations in the ordinary somatic cells of the body. Most mutations which occur spontaneously in germ cells are deleterious, and the germ cells of older animals carry more mutations than those of young animals. If similar deleterious mutations occur and accumulate in somatic cells, then they would be expected to make the cells, and eventually the whole animal, less and less efficient. Implicit or explicit in most versions of the theory is the idea that it is primarily the mutations occurring in non-dividing non-replaceable cells which are important. Mutations in cells in actively dividing tissues such as the epidermis are less important, because they can be replaced by new cells. In nerve or muscle tissue on the other hand, cells are not replaced so there would, according to the somatic mutation theory, be a gradual but inevitable deterioration of these tissues.

The somatic mutation theories had their origin in the observation that ionizing radiation, a very potent mutagenic agent, is one of the most effective ways of shortening the life of experimental animals. We have already considered the acute lethal effects of ionizing radiation (page 17). At lower doses irradiated animals show no obvious immediate effects after irradia-

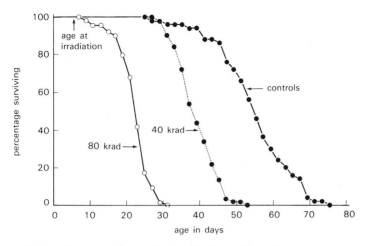

Figure 5.5 Survival curves for irradiated male *Drosophila melanogaster*.

tion, but there is usually a long-term life-shortening effect. Figure 5.5 shows a series of survival curves for male *D. melanogaster* which were given a single sub-lethal dose of gamma-radiation early in life. There is a clear shifting of the survival curves to the left as dose increases. Similar results have been obtained in many other species.

Figure 5.6 shows dose-response curves for the mouse and for *D. melanogaster*. The exact relation between dose and the amount of life-shortening is a matter of some dispute, and undoubtedly depends not only on the type of ionizing radiation and dose rate, but also on the strain and age of the animals used, and on the environmental conditions in which they are maintained. In a number of experiments with insects (and also in a few with mice) it has been found that after relatively low doses of acute or chronic radiation, life-span is actually increased. Various explanations of this phenomenon have been proposed. For example, it has been suggested that irradiation may enhance survival chances because it kills pathogens. Alternatively, for *Drosophila* females, the prolongation of life may be due to the reduction in egg-laying caused by the radiation treatment. This idea is supported by the fact that no increase in longevity is found following irradiation of genetically sterile females. However, since it has been reported that the life-span of male flies is also sometimes increased after irradiation, factors other than egg-laying must also be involved.

Although relatively low doses prolong the life of a few species, exposure to ionizing radiation usually shortens the life-span. Even *Paramecium* shows

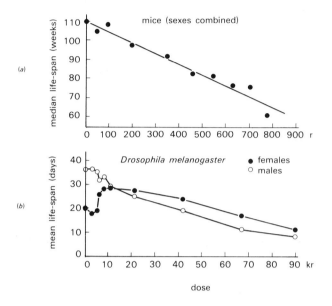

Figure 5.6 Dose-survival relations for (*a*) inbred mice irradiated with a single dose of X-rays when 30 days old (redrawn from Lindop and Rotblat, 1961), and (*b*) *Drosophila melanogaster* irradiated with a single dose of X-rays when 1 day old (based on data of Nöthel, *Strahlentherapie*, **126**, 269, 1965).

an accelerated decline in fission rate and reduced clonal life-span after irradiation. In mammals irradiation increases the incidence of malignant disease, but the life-shortening effect is not simply due to this. Analysis of the cause of death in irradiated mice has shown that they usually die from the same spectrum of diseases as their unirradiated contemporaries, although the relative frequencies of the different causes of death may not be the same.

What is the cause of radiation-induced life-shortening? Does irradiation shorten the life-span because it causes somatic mutations? Is natural ageing due to the accumulation of somatic mutations? One of the difficulties of testing the somatic mutation theory is that it is very difficult to identify and quantify somatic mutations in most cell types. Curtis (1966) and his co-workers have shown that one type of somatic mutation (chromosome aberrations in liver cells) does increase with age, and that the number of this type of mutation is increased after irradiation (see chapter 6). However, quantitatively the relation between the number of aberrations and the amount of life-shortening produced by a given dose is not what would be predicted by the somatic mutation theory. A dose of X-radiation which has very little life-shortening effect produces many more aberrations than would be necessary to explain the life-shortening it produces.

One of the main reasons why the somatic mutation theory of ageing is now less popular than it once was is that it has proved very difficult to reconcile it with the observed quantitative relations between dose of radiation and the amount of life-shortening produced. For example, if ionizing radiation shortens life because it causes somatic mutations, a large number of assumptions has to be made to explain the relative sensitivities of male and female *Habrobracon*, and of diploid and triploid *Drosophila*. *Habrobracon* is a parasitic wasp in which normal males are haploid and females are diploid. In spite of the fact that females have two copies of each gene and males have only one, their life-spans are similar. Furthermore, although males are more sensitive to the life-shortening effects of radiation, they are not really sensitive enough for deleterious recessive mutations to be the cause of the life-shortening. Similarly, with *D. melanogaster*, if somatic mutations cause radiation-induced life-shortening, it is difficult to see why males, normal diploid females, and triploid females should all show similar relative amounts of life-shortening following a given dose. Males have one less X-chromosome than normal females, and triploid females have three copies of each chromosome instead of the usual two, yet they are equally sensitive to the life-shortening effects of radiation. As Lamb and Maynard Smith (1964, 1965) have shown, these data cannot really be reconciled with a simple somatic mutation hypothesis.

If the somatic mutation theory is correct, then chemical mutagens as well as ionizing radiation should have life-shortening effects. It has been shown by Alexander (1966) and others that, although some chemical mutagens do indeed shorten life, others such as ethyl methane sulphonate (EMS), which is a very potent mutagen, do not produce any detectable life-shortening. If mutations cause ageing, why doesn't EMS shorten the life-span?

A few studies have been made of the biochemical, physiological and pathological changes which occur in irradiated animals as they get older. The results have been ambiguous, with some studies suggesting that ageing changes do occur earlier in irradiated animals, others that they do not. The ability to withstand stresses such as toxic chemicals or very high doses of radiation, declines more rapidly in irradiated animals than in controls, but age-related changes in collagen are unaffected. Alexander compared the histopathological changes in serially killed irradiated and normal mice, but found no evidence of accelerated or precocious changes in those which had been irradiated.

Awareness of the life-shortening effects of ionizing radiation in experimental animals has led to a search for similar effects in human populations which have been exposed to radiation either accidentally or therapeutically. Studies have been made of radiologists, of people receiving high doses of radiation during medical treatment, of the Marshall Islands population which was accidently exposed to radioactive fall-out in 1954, and of the survivors of the atomic bombs dropped at Nagasaki and Hiroshima (see Anderson, 1973). Conflicting evidence about the effects of radiation on longevity and ageing has come from these studies. Some investigators have claimed that the age-specific death rates of early radiologists are higher than those of appropriate control groups, but this conclusion has been disputed. It is in any case rather difficult to evaluate the actuarial data that are available. The early radiologists probably received a considerable exposure to X-rays in the years before it was realized how harmful ionizing radiation could be, but it is difficult to estimate the size of the dose that they received, and also to find an appropriate control group with which to compare them.

With the Marshall Islands population, the time since exposure is at present too short to expect any significant long-term effect on mortality to be apparent. Tests have been made on the exposed people to try to assess whether any significant acceleration in hair greying, skin elasticity changes, blood pressure changes or other physiological functions have taken place. No evidence of accelerated changes has been found. Fortunately relatively few people were involved in the accidental exposure, so the number of people in the study of after-effects is quite small. Therefore, even though they received a high dose of gamma-rays (estimated 175 rad), the tests used to assess physiological age may have been insufficiently sensitive to detect accelerated ageing in such a small sample.

The atomic bomb survivors of Hiroshima and Nagasaki form a large group of people, and many of them are being examined and tested at regular intervals. Although the studied sample is relatively large, it is not an ideal one for studying the effects of radiation on ageing. It contains relatively few men who were young or middle-aged at the time of exposure, since many of these people were in the armed forces at the time. Those who remained because they were excluded from military service probably form a very biased sample of the age-group. Mortality statistics for the people who survived the acute radiation effects show that the incidence of leukemia and other malignant diseases is higher than in a normal population, but it is still not clear whether or not the overall mortality from other causes is higher among the bomb survivors. Studies of physiological and morphological changes have so far provided no evidence to suggest that ageing processes have been accelerated in the irradiated people.

Thus, although there is a very extensive literature on the effects of radiation on man and other animals, it is difficult to draw any general conclusions about the cause of the life-shortening effect. It seems unlikely that the simple somatic mutation theory is applicable to natural ageing or to radiation-induced life-shortening. It also seems unlikely that acute doses of radiation lead to accelerated or precocious ageing in the way illustrated in figure 5.1 B or C. Nevertheless, exposure to ionizing radiation is one of the most effective ways of shortening the life of animals, and there are sufficient parallels between radiation-induced life-shortening and natural ageing to make it seem likely that at least some of the damage caused by radiation is related to that which accumulates during natural ageing.

CHAPTER SIX

AGEING OF CELLS AND TISSUES *IN VIVO*

WHAT TYPES OF CHANGE OCCUR IN THE CELLS AND TISSUES OF THE BODY AS AN animal ages? Which of the changes that can be seen cause the decline in the functional capacity of the whole animal?

It is relatively easy to detect differences between the cells of old and young animals. Deciding on their significance is far less easy. One of the difficulties is that of distinguishing between changes which are intrinsic to the cell or tissue (and may therefore cause the deterioration of the whole animal) and those which are due to the environment in which the cells are situated (and may therefore be caused by changes occurring elsewhere in the animal). For example, if a change is detected in the brain, is it the cause of the reduced efficiency of other parts of the body, or is it the consequence of the declining competence of the circulatory system in providing it with oxygen and nutrients?

In this chapter we shall consider some of the tissue and cell changes which occur as animals get older, and also the ways in which people have attempted to find out whether they are intrinsic to the cells and tissues, or whether they are the consequences of the deterioration of other parts of the body. Most of our discussion will be about mammals, since cell and tissue changes have been studied more extensively in mammals than in any other group of animals.

6.1 Types of cell and tissue

During the course of development, cells become specialized for different functions. When we look at tissues and organs in mature mammals, it is apparent that some cells are highly specialized, whereas others remain relatively undifferentiated. Also, some cells are capable of mitotic division, whereas others are not. There are a number of different schemes of classifying the cell types in the body but, for our present purposes, it is convenient to use a rather simple one based on both the extent of differentiation and the capacity of the cells to divide.

Fixed post-mitotic cells are the final products of differentiation. They are highly specialized for particular functions and are incapable of cell division. Nerve, muscle and red blood cells are examples of this cell type.

Reverting post-mitotic cells are also highly specialized but, although they are fully differentiated, they are still capable of division. Usually they do not divide frequently, but they can do so. Examples of this cell type are liver and kidney cells.

Stem cells are less specialized cells which readily undergo cell division. They are not "undifferentiated" since their fates are considerably restricted. The basal cells of the epidermis come into this category; they divide repeatedly, and the products of division differentiate into keratinized skin cells. In order to distinguish this type of cell which is in fact "partially differentiated" rather than "undifferentiated" from true embryonic totipotent cells, some people prefer the term *progenitor cell* to stem cell.

The distinction between these cell types is certainly not absolute, since not all cells fit neatly into one of these three categories. It is possible for a particular cell to be classified as a stem cell at the beginning of its life history, a reverting post-mitotic at a later stage, and ultimately as a fixed post-mitotic. Thus in the epidermis the cells in the basal layer are mitotically-active relatively-unspecialized cells. They are progenitor or stem cells. As the products of division are moved out towards the surface of the skin, keratin synthesis begins and the cells start to differentiate into specialized epidermal cells. However, although the cells which have moved out from the basal layer do not normally divide, cells in the lower part of the epidermis can in some circumstances (e.g. following a skin wound) revert to the mitotic state again. These cells might therefore be classified as reverting post-mitotics. As the cells reach the surface layers of the epidermis, they become fully differentiated and are incapable of division. They are therefore classed as fixed post-mitotics.

The different tissues and organs of the body vary with regard to the types of cell found in them. Some tissues such as the epidermis, intestinal epithelium or haemopoietic tissue are constantly being renewed. In these *renewable tissues* cell division occurs in a growth zone and as the products of division move away from the germinative region they differentiate and mature. Ultimately the fully differentiated cells die and are sloughed off or are destroyed. In the case of the skin epidermal cells they are not really fully functional until they are dead.

Tissues such as the liver do not seem to contain stem cells. Normally cell division is rare but, if cells are damaged or destroyed, the differentiated cells are capable of dividing and restoring the tissue. This type of tissue which is made up mainly of reverting post-mitotic cells is sometimes referred to as an *expanding tissue.*

Striated muscle and nervous tissue are *non-renewable tissues*, since they contain mainly fixed post-mitotic cells. If the tissues are damaged or partially destroyed, there is no reserve of partially differentiated stem cells to replace cells which are lost or defective, and the cells remaining are themselves incapable of division.

It is clear that the questions about the ageing of tissues which a gerontologist is going to ask depend to some extent on the type of tissue being studied. For renewable tissues we would like to know:

(i)   What determines the life-span of the fully differentiated cells?
(ii) Does the number of stem cells change with age?
(iii) Is there any age-dependent change in the ability of stem cells to divide?
(iv) Are newly differentiated cells in old animals as good as those in young animals?

For an expanding tissue, relevant questions might be:

(i)   Does the ability of a cell to divide depend on the time since it last divided?
(ii) Does the ability of a cell to divide depend on the animal's age?
(iii) Are there structural or biochemical changes in the cells or tissue as the animal ages?

For a non-renewable tissue we might ask:

(i)   Is there a reduction in the number of cells as the animal gets older?
(ii) Are old cells as efficient as young cells?

Some of the questions that can be asked apply to all types of cell and tissue, but for convenience we will discuss the ageing of cells and tissues *in vivo* by considering some of the studies which have been made of cells in the three types of tissue that have been described.

6.2   Ageing changes in renewing tissues

Tissues which are continually turning over might not be thought to be important in ageing, since defective or dead cells can be replaced. However, there is ample evidence to show that age-related changes do occur in the cells of these tissues. For example, it has been found for a number of tissues that the stem cell generation time is different in old and young animals.

The mitotic cycle is conventionally divided into four phases:

mitosis (M)
the pre-synthesis gap (G₁)
the synthesis stage during which new DNA is synthesized (S)
the post-synthesis gap (G₂) which precedes mitosis.

If animals are injected with tritiated thymidine, a radioactively-labelled nucleoside which is incorporated into replicating DNA, cells which are in or are about to enter S-phase at the time of injection incorporate the labelled molecules. Unless thymidine is incorporated into DNA, it is broken down and lost from the body within a short time after injection. Thus, by injecting animals with radioactive thymidine, it is possible to label a cohort of cells which were in S-phase at the time of injection. By killing animals at various times after injection, and examining their tissues using an autoradiographic technique to locate the sites of the labelled molecules, it is possible to follow the fate of this labelled cohort of cells.

Using this technique the cell generation time and movements of cells in a number of renewable tissues have been studied. Lesher and his colleagues (see Lesher and Sacher, 1968) have made extensive studies of the intestinal mucosa of mice. The stem cells for this tissue are located in the crypts of Lieberkühn, where active mitotic division can be seen. Newly formed cells are pushed out from the crypts onto the villus, where they gradually pass to the tip and ultimately drop off. Figure 6.1 shows the percentage of labelled mitotic figures found in the crypt cells of mice of different ages at various intervals after injection with tritiated thymidine. The stem cells do not form a synchronous population, so only a proportion of the cells were in S-phase during the time when tritiated thymidine was available for incorporation into the DNA. Animals which were killed $\frac{1}{2}$ hour after injection showed no labelled mitotic figures, because the cells undergoing mitosis were in G_2 at the time of injection. Gradually, however, $\frac{1}{2}$-2 hours after injection, mitotic figures were found to be labelled because the labelled cohort of cells which were in S-phase began to undergo mitotic division. Between 2 and 7–9 hours, all of the cells which showed mitotic figures were labelled, i.e. all of the dividing cells were from the cohort of cells which was in S-phase when the animal was injected. In the following 3–4 hours, the number of labelled mitotic figures fell because the cells which were in G_1 or M at the time of injection entered mitosis. There was then a gradual increase in the percentage of labelled mitoses as the cohort of labelled cells began its second division.

By looking at the time between corresponding points on the curves for the first and second waves of mitoses, it is possible to calculate the length of the complete mitotic cycle, i.e. the cell generation time. Estimates of the time spent in the different phases of the cycle can be calculated from the slopes of the ascending and descending limbs of the curves, and the levels and positions of the plateaus and troughs.

The figure shows that as mice get older there is an increase in the cell

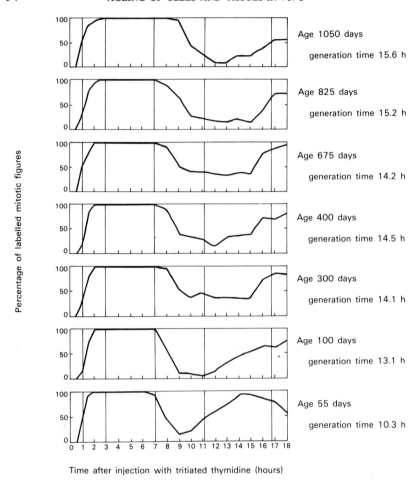

Figure 6.1 Percentage of labelled mitotic figures and estimated generation time for duodenal crypt cells in mice of different ages (redrawn from Lesher and Sacher, 1968).

generation time. The biggest increase occurs as the juveniles become mature. There is little change between 300 and 675 days of age, but in old animals the generation time again increases. This increase in generation time is largely due to an increase in the amount of time that the cells spend in G_1 and S.

In addition to the studies of cell generation time, Lesher and his colleagues have shown that the transit time of cells from the crypts to the extrusion zone increases with age, and that the number of crypt cells which are dividing decreases from 132 cells per crypt in 100-day-old mice to 92 cells per crypt in 825-day-old mice. They estimate that the decrease in the number of proliferating cells, combined with the increased generation time in old animals, means that the rate of production of new epithelial cells is 50% less than in a 3-month-old mouse. Since there is no evidence of a decrease in the number of cells in the villi as the animal ages, this means that the life-span of newly formed epithelial cells must be greater in old animals.

What determines the longevity of the differentiated cells in the villi and the mitotic rate of the stem cells in the crypts? Are cell cycle-times and cell life-spans increased because the stem cells themselves are showing ageing changes, or do they vary as a result of changes in the extracellular environment (e.g. hormone levels or the efficiency of the vascular supply)? There is reason to believe that the stem cells are capable of faster mitotic rates than are normally found in old animals. In mice which are subjected to low levels of continuous irradiation, the length of the cell cycle is considerably reduced even in old animals. This is presumably a compensatory reaction to produce new cells to replace those which are damaged by radiation. The fact that in old animals the mitotic rate can be accelerated suggests that the increased generation time which occurs in normal ageing does not occur as a result of changes in the stem cells themselves.

The whole problem of what determines the mitotic rate of stem cells and the longevity of differentiated cells is an intriguing one. In an adult mammal, the rates of cell formation and cell loss must be delicately balanced. If they were not, there would be changes in the mass of organs and tissues. When the stem cell mitotic rate is high, as in the intestinal crypts, the life expectancy of the differentiated cells must be short. When the mitotic rate is moderate, as in the basal cells of the epidermis, the life-span of the differentiated cells must also be moderate. In tissues such as the liver, where mitotic rate is normally very low, the functional cells must be very long-lived.

Bullough (1967) has argued that the balance between cell loss and cell gain is maintained because both the mitotic rate and the rate of cell ageing depend on chalone control systems. Chalones are tissue-specific mitotic inhibitors which are synthesized within the cells of the tissues on which they act. Their action in inhibiting mitosis is enhanced by adrenalin and glucocorticoid hormones. When chalone concentration falls, cells enter mitosis; when it is high, mitosis is inhibited and cells enter what Bullough calls the "ageing pathway" which leads to functional maturity and ultimately death. Bullough believes that chalone action determines not only the mitotic rate in tissues, but also the life-expectancy of the cells. He has pointed out that, when mice are stressed by partial starvation, the mitotic rate in the epidermis is greatly reduced, yet the thickness of the epidermis is not decreased. This must mean that the rate of cell loss is also lower than in normal animals, i.e. the cells have a longer life-span. Conversely, it has been shown that in psoriasis where epidermal mitotic rate is greatly increased, the life-span of the cells is reduced from 14-21 days to only 4 days. Thus cell life-expectancy and mitotic rate are closely correlated – within any one tissue life-span is inversely proportional to mitotic rate. Figure 6.2 shows the relation between mitotic rate and life-span for sebaceous gland cells in rats where the mitotic rate varied as a result of castration, hypophysectomy, and testosterone injection.

If it is accepted that chalone concentration controls both the rate of mitosis and cell life-span, does it do so because mitotic rate itself determines cell life-expectancy, or because chalones have two separate actions, one on the mitotic rate and one on the rate of ageing? Is cell life-span determined by the length of the mitotic cycle when it was formed? Bullough argues that it is not because, when chalone concentration is changed, not only is mitotic rate in the stem cells changed, but the life-span of cells which have already

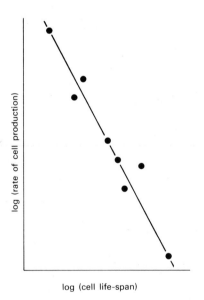

log (cell life-span)

Figure 6.2   Relation between the life-span and mitotic rate of rat sebaceous gland cells (redrawn from Bullough, 1967).

differentiated is also altered. Therefore chalones affect the mitotic cycle and cell life-span independently.

Bullough (1973) speculated that in non-renewable tissues, such as the brain and muscle, chalone concentration is very high and hence the cells age very slowly. Since it is known that in renewing tissues, stress hormones enhance chalone action, he suggested that stress may lead to an increased life-span if non-dividing cells (such as nerve cells) are the pacemakers for ageing changes. Enhanced chalone action due to stress hormones could mean that fixed post-mitotic cells age more slowly. He suggested that the experiments in which the life-spans of mammals were increased by food restriction could be interpreted in these terms, since one of the effects of food restriction is to increase the size of the adrenals. Adrenalin enhances chalone action and therefore, according to Bullough's hypothesis, it could decrease the rate of post-mitotic cell ageing, and thus increase the life-span of the mammals.

All of the renewable tissues which have been mentioned so far are ones in which the stem cells and fully differentiated cells remain in close proximity. There are other types of renewable "tissues", e.g. the blood cells in the circulatory system, in which the final products of differentiation do not remain closely associated with the stem cells. It could be argued that, in tissues such as the epidermis or gut epithelium, the life-span of the cells is determined by their position in the tissue. This cannot be true for cells such as red blood cells, which are derived from stem cells in the bone marrow. Nevertheless, there is good evidence showing that red blood cells do show actuarial senescence, i.e. their destruction by macrophages is not a random process, but the likelihood of being destroyed increases as they get older. This has been shown by labelling a cohort of cells with radioactive chromium, injecting these cells into host animals, and following the loss of chromium from the blood. In man, the average erythrocyte life-span is about 120 days; in the rat it is about half this value. During the life-span of red cells there are changes in enzyme activity, cell density, osmotic fragility and mechanical properties. Recently Kay (1975) has shown that senescent red cells seemed to be recognized and destroyed by macrophages because, although young cells are recognized as "self" by macrophages, immunoglobulins in serum attach to the surface of old cells, thereby preventing the macrophages from recognizing them as "self". Since they are no longer recognized as "self", the old cells are phagocytized.

Erythrocytes undoubtedly show senescence but, unlike the duodenal crypt cells discussed earlier, there is no reason to think that their life-span depends on the age of the animal. This has been shown by taking radioactively-labelled cells from young and old donor animals and following their fate in young and old hosts. The results showed that the cell life-spans are not affected by the age of the animal which produced them, or by the age of the animal which provides their environment. However, although the life-spans of red cells seem to be unaffected by the animal's age, there is evidence that the quality of the cells may be different in old animals. For example, Silini and Andreozzi (1974) have reported that there are small changes in haematocrit, and that haemoglobin concentration in mouse erythrocytes decreases slightly with age. The causes of these changes are not clear.

Studying the mitotic rate and size of the stem cell population for erythrocytes is much more difficult than it is for epidermal or gut mucosal cells, and most attempts to determine whether or not blood-cell-forming tissue undergoes changes with age have been indirect. For example, Grant and LeGrande (1964) attempted to assess erythropoietic changes with age by measuring the level of circulating erythrocytes in rats which were kept at reduced atmospheric pressure or which had been made anaemic by removing a known amount of blood. Both of these treatments stimulate the bone marrow to produce new red cells. They found that old rats took about twice as long as young rats to restore the red-cell level to normal after bleeding, and that in low oxygen tensions the number of circulating red cells did not increase to the same extent in old animals as it did in young. This may mean that there is an age-related decrease in the ability of the bone marrow stem cells to produce new erythrocytes, but the change could also be the result of a deterioration in the efficiency of the feed-back control system which regulates red-cell production. For example, the production of erythropoietin, the hormone formed in the kidney which is responsible for stimulating stem cells to differentiate, might be less efficient in old animals.

Another technique which has been used to assess the proliferative capacity of bone-marrow cells involves measuring their ability to form colonies in the spleens of irradiated mice. When mice are exposed to a high dose of radiation, their own proliferative cells are destroyed. If bone-marrow cells from another animal are suspended and a known concentration is injected into the irradiated host animal, some of the cells lodge in the spleen and divide to form small colonies which can be detected and counted. The number of colony-forming units (CFUs) relative to the number of cells injected gives an estimate of the proliferative capacity of marrow cells. The results obtained using this technique have been contradictory. For example, Coggle and Proukakis (1970) found no age-related change in the proportion of CFUs for mouse-femur marrow cells. They also estimated that the total number of nucleated bone-marrow cells did not change with age, and hence that there was no change in the overall proliferative capacity of the blood-- forming tissue. Silini and Andreozzi (1974), on the other hand, found that femur marrow cells showed a decreased ability to form spleen colonies as age increased, but that there was an increase in the number of marrow cells in the femur. Although the results were different, both of these studies suggest that there is probably no substantial change in the proliferative potential of the bone marrow with increasing age. It must be remembered, however, that the bone-marrow cells are pluripotential stem cells which can give rise to cells committed to granulocyte, thrombocyte and lymphocyte production as well as to erythrocytes. Even if the bone marrow cells are still capable of proliferation, it does not mean that the capacity of old and young animals to produce erythrocytes is necessarily the same.

6.3   Ageing in the liver, an expanding tissue

In the liver, cell division is normally very rare; only about one in every 10-20 thousand cells is in mitosis at any instant. Although there is no stem cell population, the liver retains the ability to replace damaged or lost cells. Extensive cell loss results in a rapid increase in the rate of mitosis. If the two main lobes of a rat liver are removed, the cells in the remaining one third of the liver divide and restore the tissue to its original mass within about 2 weeks.

Bucher (1963) has compared the ability of old and young rats to regenerate lost liver following partial hepatectomy. She found that, although old animals were quite capable of restoring liver mass, age certainly affected regeneration. Figure 6.3 shows the results obtained when she followed the time course of DNA synthesis in the liver of partially hepatectomized rats of different ages. Rats from which two thirds of the liver had been removed were injected with a radioactive DNA precursor at intervals after the opera- tion. Two hours later the amount of radioactive label incorporated into the liver was measured. The curves show that in young animals DNA synthesis began within 16 hours of operation and reached a peak after 22 hours. This peak was followed by a trough as most of the cells moved into G_2 and M-phase. There was then a second peak at 35 hours as another population of cells entered S-phase. In older animals the regenerative response was different. Firstly, there was a longer lag before DNA synthesis was initiated, indicating that the rate of cell replacement was probably slower. Secondly, there was a more gradual increase in DNA synthesis and a single less-- distinct peak. This suggests that the cell population was less synchronous

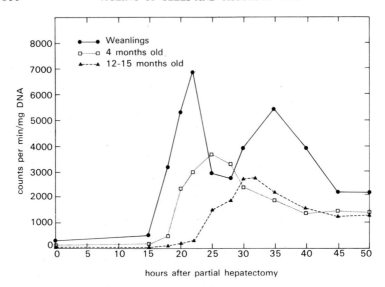

Figure 6.3 Liver regeneration in rats after partial hepatectomy. DNA synthesis was measured by finding the amount of radioactively labelled thymidine incorporated in a 2-hour period (redrawn from Bucher, 1963).

than in young animals. In addition, Bucher has shown that old rats are less tolerant of liver loss than young animals – a 10% liver loss in old animals produces the same kind of response as a 40% loss in young animals.

It is not clear why the liver shows differences in regenerative responses as the animal gets older, but in normal animals (where the liver cells rarely divide) a number of age-related changes in structure and function have been reported, and some of these may be associated with the changing regenerative responses. Among the most interesting changes are those occurring in the cell nuclei. First of all, there is an increase in the number of polyploid nuclei as animals get older. Secondly, the number of chromosome abnormalities increases. This observation was referred to in the last chapter while considering the somatic mutation theories of ageing. Curtis and his colleagues (see Curtis 1966) were able to measure the frequency of chromosome aberrations by exploiting the regenerative capacity of the liver. They destroyed part of the liver of mice by injecting carbon tetrachloride subcutaneously. Three days after injection, when active liver regeneration and cell divisions were occurring, the mice were killed, the livers were removed, and the tissue was examined microscopically. Cells in which the later stages of mitosis were visible were scored as either normal or abnormal. Abnormal cells were those which showed either chromosome "fragments" which were not taking part in the normal movements of mitosis, or "bridges" between the separating chromosomes, indicating that the division was abnormal. The results from one of Curtis's experiments in which he compared the changes in the proportions of chromosome aberrations in two inbred mouse strains are shown in figure 6.4 In both strains, chromosome aberration frequency increased with age, but the rate of increase was greater in the short-lived strain. In dogs, Curtis found that the rate of increase was much slower than in mice; so overall there was a tendency for the rate of increase in aberrations to be lower in long-lived animals. However, although these results show that chromosome mutations increase with age and that the rate of increase is correlated with the longevity of the strain or species, the large increase in aberration frequency which is produced by a small dose of ionizing radiation makes it difficult to accept the results as conclusive evidence in favour of the somatic mutation theory of ageing. Nevertheless, the data do show that, during normal ageing, liver cells accumulate chromosome damage. It is not unreasonable to suppose that this damage may affect regenerative capacity and the general functional ability of the liver.

Adelman (1972) has found that some functional changes in the liver depend on the age of the animal rather than the age of the cells. He has made

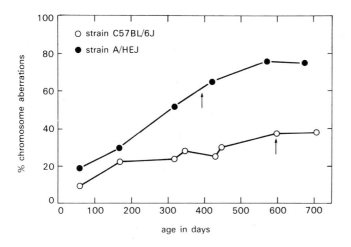

Figure 6.4 Age-related changes in the numbers of chromosome aberrations in regenerating livers of two different inbred strains of mice. The arrows mark the median life-spans of each strain (redrawn from Curtis, 1966).

an extensive study of enzyme adaptation, particularly in the liver. When nutritional, physiological or pharmacological stimuli are given to an animal, part of the adaptive response to the stimulus involves an alteration in the level of activity of certain enzymes. For example, in the rat liver the activity of glucokinase, the enzyme which initially activates glucose, is high in fully fed rats, decreases by as much as 90% after 3 days of fasting, but returns to the original level within a day or so of re-feeding with glucose. Insulin is necessary for this adaptive response to occur. Adelman has shown that there is an age-dependent decrease in the ability of rats to respond to the changes in diet. With increasing age there is an increase in the time taken for the recovery response following re-feeding to begin (figure 6.5). Consequently, whereas young rats take only one day to restore the initial enzyme level, old rats take two or more days. Similar age-related increases in the lag period before response have been found for cytochrome *c* reductase and tyrosine aminotransferase in response to phenobarbital and ACTH respectively. Of particular interest is Adelman's observation that in old rats which

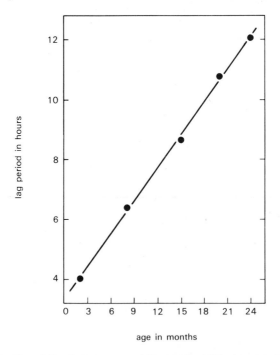

Figure 6.5   The relation between age and the duration of the lag period of glucokinase induction in the rat liver (redrawn from Adelman, *Exp. Gerontol.*, **6**, 75, 1971).

had been partially hepatectomized, the fully regenerated livers showed exactly the same delayed enzyme induction as livers in normal animals of the same age. The response of new cells on old animals was the same as the response of old cells in old animals. This suggests that the age-dependent modifications of enzyme adaptation are consequences of either genetic changes which are inherited by the new cells produced during regeneration, or changes in some part of the body other than the liver cells themselves. Since increase in glucokinase activity following injection of insulin is not altered during ageing, it seems likely that the age-related changes in enzyme regulation in the liver may be associated with changes in the hormonal control mechanisms rather than changes in the liver cells themselves.

6.4 Ageing in non-renewable tissues

Brain and skeletal muscle are the classic examples of tissues in which there is no cell replacement throughout adult life. Many people believe that changes in this type of tissue may be the primary cause of most of the functional deterioration which occurs during ageing. In particular, because of its importance in integrating body functions, nervous tissue has for a long time been thought of as a likely candidate for the role of pacemaker in ageing processes. Muscle atrophy is a well-known symptom of old age, and it has been shown that accompanying a decrease in muscle weight there is a loss of muscle fibres. However, neuronal and hormonal factors can have profound effects on muscle, so it is very difficult to know whether the loss of muscular strength and the visible changes in muscle structure which accompany increasing age are the results of intrinsic changes in the muscle tissue itself or are results of alterations in the nervous and endocrine systems.

Although everyone knows that in man many brain cells die every day, the evidence on which this popular belief is based is really not at all substantial. The first suggestion that nerve cells are lost as we get older came from Hodge at the end of the last century. He counted nerve cells in the brains of the honey bee and man, and detected an age-related reduction in the number of cells in each. Since that time data both supporting and contradicting this observation have been reported. Recently Corsellis (1975) has reviewed much of the literature on the subject and has presented new data based on counting cells in sections of brain tissue from a large number of normal humans. He concluded that there is evidence of cell loss. His own data showed that the Purkinje cells of the cerebellum decrease in number by about 25% between the ages of 1 and 100 years.

For the mouse, Johnson and Erner (1972) have made estimates of the total number of neuronal cells in the brain. They were able to form a cell suspension of the entire brain by using sonication to separate the cells after the brains had been fixed in formalin. Although they found that there was little change in the number of glial cells, the neurone population fell from over 5 million in young mice to 2 million in extreme old age. The rate of loss of neurones increased as age increased, the largest loss occurring in the last few months of life. This seems to be good evidence for cell loss, but as Franks (1974) has pointed out, one possible reason for the apparent cell loss found when using sonication techniques to estimate cell numbers is that old neurones may be more fragile and therefore more likely to be destroyed by sonication. Franks cites evidence which shows that there is no loss in the total amount of DNA in the brain of rats. If cell loss is extensive, the amount of DNA should decrease. Since it does not, Franks is doubtful that cell loss is as extensive as some studies suggest.

Although the evidence for generalized cell loss in the ageing brain is still not conclusive, there is no doubt that there are very distinct changes in the appearance of neural tissues in a number of animals. The most striking visible change is the accumulation of lipofuscin or age pigment. This pigment accumulates in the cytoplasm of a number of different cells, particularly the long-lived non-mitotic cells in non-renewable tissues such as muscle or nervous tissue. However, it is not limited to non-dividing cells, since it is also found in the liver, spleen, pancreas, thymus, gonads, and some other tissues. It also occurs in a variety of non-mammalian animals, e.g. leeches, snails, protozoans, insects. Within any one species, similar cells in different parts of the body may accumulate the pigment at different rates.

Lipofuscin in nerve or muscle cells appears as small yellow or brown granules sometimes spread throughout the cytoplasm, but often clustered around the nucleus or at one pole. It binds a number of fat-soluble stains and shows autofluorescence. Ultrastructural studies have shown that the lipofuscin granules may be bounded by a single membrane and sometimes have a laminate structure. However, their appearance is very variable, even within the same cell type. Their biochemical properties suggest that they have a lipoprotein origin.

Figure 6.6 shows the age-dependent accumulation of lipofuscin in human myocardium. Quite clearly there is a good correlation between age and the amount of pigment. Similar observations on the myocardium of the dog show that the rate of accumulation is more rapid than in man.

The amount of lipofuscin present in particular tissues is such a good indicator of chronological age that there has been quite extensive study of the pigment and considerable speculation about its origin and functional impor-

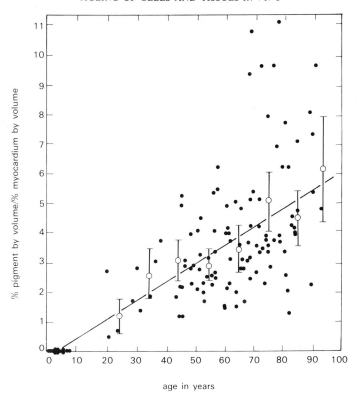

Figure 6.6 The relationship between age and lipofuscin content of human myocardium (redrawn from Strehler, 1962).

tance. In spite of the large amount of structural and biochemical data available, the origin of age pigment is still obscure (Toth, 1968). A number of people have suggested that lipofuscin is derived from mitochondria. However, the enzymes found associated with lipofuscin granules are not the same as those found associated with mitochondria and, when present, the granule membrane is not the same as that of mitochondria. The general consensus of opinion seems to be that lipofuscin granules are more likely to be derived from lysosomes. Lysosomes are small cytoplasmic organelles with a single membrane and high levels of proteolytic enzyme activity. They play an important role in intracellular digestion and waste removal. It is suggested that since lysosomes have poor lipolytic activity, age pigment granules may be the residue left after lysosome activity. Vitamin E deficiency and prolonged hyperoxia both increase the rate of lipofuscin production. Since both conditions also increase the formation of free radicals which can cause peroxidation and polymerization of unsaturated fatty acids in organelle membranes, it may be that the increase in age pigment accumulation is a consequence of the damage to membranes in cells. Possibly some pigment granules are formed when lysosomes engulf damaged membranes.

The effect of lipofuscin granules on the functional capacities of cells is not known. They may simply be indicators of the results of cell damage, but on the other hand the accumulation of lipofuscin may itself eventually impair the ability of cells to function normally. The granules could affect transport or diffusion of materials through the cell, although in most cells and tissues the volume of space that they occupy is relatively small.

6.5 Transplantation experiments

It should be clear from the discussion in the preceding sections that it is very difficult to decide whether a particular age-related change is an intrinsic property of the particular cell or tissue being studied, or whether it is a consequence of changes in the environment provided by old and young animals. Attempts have been made to separate the effects of the age of the cells and tissues from the age of the animal by transplantation experiments. In principle these experiments are quite straightforward. For example, in order to see whether cells are capable of indefinite proliferation, cells are taken from an old animal and transplanted into a young host; as the host becomes old, the descendants of the original cells are re-transplanted into a fresh young host, and so on. Using this serial transplantation technique, it should be possible to see whether a particular cell line has a limited life-span or not. A comparable technique can be used to see whether the tissue age or the animal age determines some change in function: cells or tissues from an old animal can be put into a young host and *vice versa.*

Although superficially these experiments seem to be straightforward, there are many technical and interpretive difficulties. First of all it is essential that donor and host should be genetically similar in order to avoid the possibility of an immunological reaction between host and graft material. Secondly, it has to be possible to distinguish host and donor material. One way of achieving this is to put the donor material into a site which it does not normally occupy. Although this facilitates the identification of donor material, it has the disadvantage that the transplanted tissue is not in its normal environment, and this may affect its function. Another method is one which has already been mentioned briefly, namely, destroying the corresponding tissue in the host before transplanting donor material. This is the technique used to assay bone-marrow stem-cell proliferation – the host is irradiated with a radiation dose sufficient to destroy its own haemopoietic cells before the donor material is injected, so that all the haemopoietic tissue is of donor origin. The disadvantage of this technique is that a heavily irradiated animal is not a normal environment for any cells or tissues, and functional changes in donor tissue could be the result of the abnormal environment. Harrison (1975) has used a technique for studying haemopoietic cell proliferation which avoids this problem by making use of genetically anaemic mice. Donor material from normal animals can be transplanted into these mice and cure the anaemia. Donor cells can be distinguished from host cells if a chromosome marker is used, i.e. the donor cell chromosomes are structurally slightly different from those of the host. Alternatively, host and donor cells can carry different haemoglobin genes, so that the activity of host and donor tissue can be distinguished by the type of haemoglobin produced.

In spite of the technical difficulties involved in transplantation experiments, it has been shown by using these techniques that many tissues can be kept alive for far longer than the normal life-span of the animal from which they came (see Daniel, 1972). Mouse skin has been kept alive for nearly 7 years by serially transplanting it to new host animals, although the grafts became smaller and were more difficult to transplant successfully as they got older. Mouse prostates have been maintained as subcutaneous grafts for 6 years, and they retained their usual structure and were probably capable of living longer.

Serial transplantation of haemopoietic cells has been carried out by injecting bone-marrow cells into irradiated hosts, allowing them to colonize the spleen and marrow, taking these cells and re-injecting them into new irradiated hosts, where they again colonized the blood-forming tissues and were available for further transplantation. Using this technique it was found that the ability of the cells to "cure" the irradiated recipient decreased with increasing numbers of transplant generations; the number of colonies formed in the spleen also decreased, but some lines were maintained for 5 years before proliferation stopped. Although this suggests that age changes did eventually occur in these lines, Harrison (1975) used genetically anaemic hosts to maintain cell lines for over 7 years. In the later transplant generations, the ability of the implanted cells to cure the host's anaemia declined, but Harrison believes that this was due to technical difficulties rather than to an intrinsic ageing process in the cell lines.

Mammary transplantation in mice has been carried out by completely removing host mammary tissue from a fat pad and replacing it with donor tissue. The transplanted material grows readily and rapidly in its natural site, but Daniel and his co-workers (see Daniel, 1972) found that growth decreased during successive transplantations, and eventually the tissue could be transplanted no more. In contrast to the decline in proliferative ability seen in normal mammary tissue, precancerous tissue could be transplanted indefinitely.

The experiments described above show that cells and tissues can survive for longer than the life-span of the animal from which they came. Nevertheless, in most experiments the transplants ultimately failed. This failure might mean that the tissue has only a limited life-span, but it could also mean that the trauma of transplantation affects it adversely. In most experiments it was found that more frequent transplantation resulted in a shorter survival time. Whether this is because frequent transfer causes more tissue damage, or because frequent transfer necessitates the cells dividing more often and hence exhausting a limited "division potential" more rapidly, is at present unresolved.

Transplantation experiments in which the effects of old and young hosts on transplanted material from old and young donors are compared have led to conflicting opinions about the relative importance of the age of the environment and the age of the cells. Using the mammary transplant system, it was found that when tissues from old and young donors were transplanted simultaneously into fat pads on opposite sides of the same young hosts, the survival times of the donor tissues were very similar (figure 6.7). When old hosts were used, none of the transplants grew very well but, on re-transplanting them to young hosts, vigorous growth was resumed. It seems likely that the hormonal environment in the old animals was inadequate to stimulate growth in the transplants. Daniel and his colleagues concluded from these experiments that *in vivo* mammary gland tissue has only a limited capacity for growth. Although the "life-spans" of old and young transplants in young hosts were similar, they argue that this is not evidence against the idea that the cells can undergo only a limited number of divisions, because it is unlikely that much cell division normally occurs in the mammary glands of mature animals. In other words, the number of mitotic divisions before transplantation was probably very similar for cells in both old and young donor material.

Harrison (1975) obtained results with bone-marrow cells which are very similar to those for mammary glands. Cells from old and young donors were almost equally effective in curing genetically anaemic mice. The cells

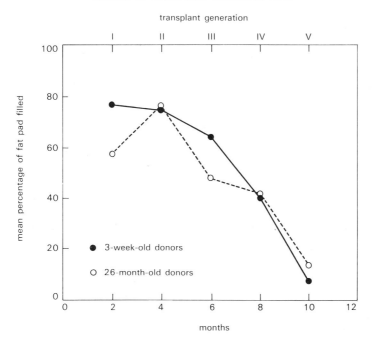

Figure 6.7 Growth of mammary transplants from young and old donors during serial passage in young hosts (redrawn from Daniel, 1972).

could be taken through the same number of transplant generations before both lines failed simultaneously. Since both lines failed at the same time, Harrison maintains that their failure was due to defects in the transplantation system rather than to the exhaustion of the proliferative capacities of the cells. His old donors were 23–30 months older than the young donors, so their marrow cells must have undergone many more doublings than those of the young animals. If cell lines die out when the cells have doubled a certain number of times, the cells from young donors should have survived longer. They did not. Thus there is no reason to ascribe the failure of either of the cell lines to an intrinsic limitation to the number of divisions that cells can undergo.

Harrison also obtained more direct evidence in favour of the idea that the defective erythropoietic response found in old animals is probably due to environmental factors rather than defects in marrow cells. As discussed previously, after severe bleeding old mice cannot restore haematocrit or haemoglobin levels to normal as quickly as young mice. Harrison found that this was still true in old animals which had received bone marrow transplants shortly before bleeding. The young marrow could not improve the response in old animals, although it could cure genetically anaemic mice in which stem cells were known to be defective. It seems likely, therefore, that the defective response in old mice is caused by environmental factors rather than by changes in their stem cells.

When considered together, the results from transplantation experiments do not provide any definite answer to the question of whether or not cells and tissues have an intrinsic ageing process independent of the ageing of the whole animal. The only tissues which have been maintained *in vivo* for very long periods are abnormal cancerous tissues. Although normal tissues and cells can be maintained for longer than the life-span of the animal from which they came, 7 years seems to be the longest survival time reported so far for mouse tissues. Since relatively few long-term experiments have been carried out, it is perhaps unwise to conclude that there is a limit to the proliferative capacity or survival time of cells and tissues *in vivo*, although some of the existing data suggest that this may be true.

6.6   Ageing of the immune system

The cells which are responsible for the immune responses, lymphocytes and macrophages, are derived from haemopoietic stem cells. They could have been considered in the general discussion of ageing in renewing tissues, but there are two good reasons for discussing the immune system separately. First of all it is known that immune responses depend on a number of different cells and tissues, and that there are complex interactions between them. The immune system therefore provides an opportunity for considering the way in which an age-related functional change depends on changes at the cellular level. Secondly, the immune system is believed by some people to be responsible for much of the deterioration and disease found in senescent vertebrates, and a number of theories have been developed which postulate that the immune system is the pacemaker for ageing changes.

Two types of immunological reaction can occur when an antigen enters the body. Some antigens stimulate the synthesis and release of humoral antibodies which are mainly involved in neutralization of bacterial toxins and destruction of bacteria. Other antigens lead to the formation of lymphocytes which are the effectors of cell-mediated reactions such as delayed hypersensitivity, or rejection of skin transplants. There are two basic types of immunocompetent lymphocytes involved in these reactions: thymus-dependent lymphocytes (T-cells) which are mainly concerned with cell-mediated immunity and thymus-independent lymphocytes (B-cells) which are involved in the production of circulating antibodies. However, for the production of many humoral antibodies it is known that the co-operation of "helper" T-cells, macrophages, and B-cells is necessary.

In the adult, both B-cells and T-cells are thought to be derived from bone-marrow stem cells. The T-cells are produced when cells from the bone-marrow implant in the thymus proliferate and differentiate into antigen-receptive cells. Eventually they pass into the blood, where they form a long-lived recirculating population of cells, many of which lodge in the spleen, lymph nodes and other lymphoid tissues. Recent evidence suggests that it may not be necessary for the thymus to come in direct contact with T-cell precursors, since the thymus secretes a hormone which influences T-cell production. In birds, the site of differentiation of B-cells is in the bursa of Fabricius, a diverticulum of the cloaca. In mammals, the site of differentiation is not known, but it is probably in the bone marrow. Once they have differentiated, immunocompetent B-cells also circulate in the blood and lodge in the lymphoid organs and tissues.

Further differentiation and proliferation of T- and B-cells depends on the presence of antigen. When they meet an appropriate antigen, they divide and differentiate to produce "memory cells" and the end-products of differentiation which in the case of B-cells are antibody-producing plasma cells, and in the case of T-cells are the effector cells for the cellular reactions and the "helper" cells for the humoral responses. Memory cells are committed cells which are responsible for the rapid response following a second contact with the same antigen.

This rather simplified account of the production of the cells involved in immune responses is shown diagrammatically in figure 6.8. The system is obviously a complex one involving at least the circulatory system, bone marrow, spleen, thymus, lymph nodes and other lymphoid tissue. There are many places where age-related deteriorations might occur.

The immune responses show very marked changes with age. Immunological capacity grows during the juvenile stages, is maximal in the young adult, and thereafter declines steadily. This can be shown in a number of ways. For example, in man, the titres of naturally-occurring anti-A and anti-B antibodies in people of blood group O decrease after the age of 10 until in old age they are only a third of their peak levels. Experimentally, Makinodan and his colleagues (see Makinodan *et al.*, 1971) have shown that in mice the primary and secondary antibody-forming activity of spleen cells decreases with age. They injected a fixed number of spleen cells from donor mice of different ages into recipients which had been heavily

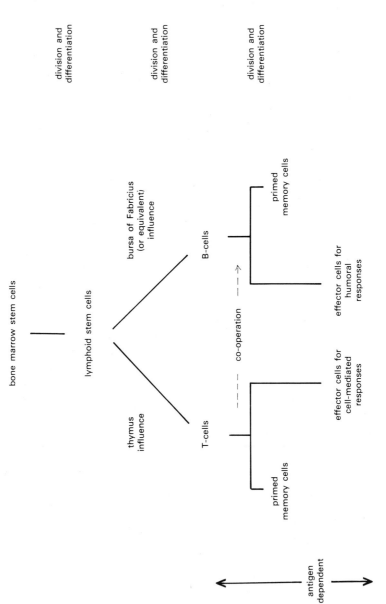

Figure 6.8 The production of the cells involved in immune responses.

irradiated so that their own lymphocytes had been destroyed. Rat red blood cells were injected at the same time to provide an antigenic stimulus. Figure 6.9 shows the results obtained when the antibody-forming ability of the hosts was measured. The primary antibody forming potential showed a marked decrease with age. The secondary antibody-forming response was measured by using donor cells from mice which had been immunized with an optimum dose of antigen when they were 4 weeks old. Although the secondary response was always higher than the primary response, it too declined with age.

Declining efficiency of the cell-mediated immune responses is more difficult to demonstrate. Allergic reactions tend to be less common in the elderly, and studies of delayed hypersensitivity reactions in old people show that they have a decreased responsiveness to antigens such as tuberculin which they had probably encountered early in life. Experimentally, there is

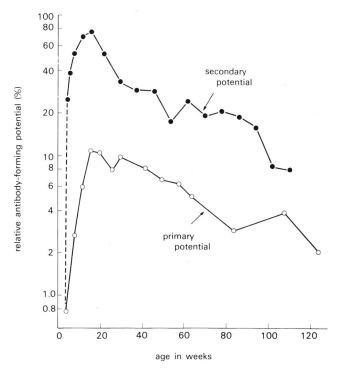

Figure 6.9   Antibody-forming activity of the spleen cells of mice of various ages (redrawn from Makinodan *et al.*, 1971).

some evidence that allografts, i.e. tissue grafts involving animals of different genetic constitutions, are rejected less readily by old mice than by young. Old mice also seem far less resistant to allogeneic tumour cells than young mice. This suggests that the cell-mediated responses also decline with age.

From figure 6.8 it is apparent that the age-related decline in immune function could be caused by defects at many different points in the development of the cells which mediate the immune responses. We have already considered evidence which suggests that the bone-marrow stem-cell pool is not seriously reduced in old animals, so it seems unlikely that the decline in the immune response is due to lack of stem cells. It is not known whether the rate of proliferation is the same in old and young animals, or whether there are age-related changes in the ability of stem-cell progeny to respond to the stimuli initiating lymphocyte precursor-cell differentiation. Little is known about the differentiation of macrophages and B-cells. However, we do know that for the development of T-cells and the cell-mediated immune reactions the thymus is essential. In mice, removal of the thymus immediately after birth leads to a reduced number of circulating lymphocytes, failure to reject allografts, and a reduction in the ability to produce humoral antibody to some antigens. Furthermore, athymic mice show changes early in life which parallel those shown in natural ageing.

Since the thymus is obviously essential for the development of the T-cell population, and athymic mice seem to show premature ageing, it is natural to think that thymus involution may be involved in the decline in the efficiency of many of the immune responses as the animal gets older. The relative size of the thymus begins to decrease soon after birth, and after puberty the absolute weight declines. Lymphoid tissue tends to be replaced by fat and fibrous tissue. The extent to which this involution of the thymus affects the capacity of the animal to produce T-cells is not known. According to Hirokawa (1975), an old thymus is less capable of promoting T-cell differentiation than a young thymus. He implanted thymic lobes of different ages into mice which had been thymectomized, irradiated to destroy their existing lymphocytes, and then injected with young marrow cells. He argued that repopulation of the spleen and lymph nodes with T-cells, and the recovery of the cellular responses dependent on functional T-cells, would occur only if the implanted thymus could effect the differentiation of T-cells. He found that grafts of thymus lobes from old animals were less capable of promoting the re-population of the lymphoid tissue with T-cells than those of young animals. With increasing age of the thymus graft, fewer T-cells were produced and some T-cell-dependent immune responses were reduced. From this it seems that old thymus glands are less efficient than young ones in producing new T-cells. However, it does not necessarily follow that the old thymus is incapable of maintaining an adequate efficient population of T-cells in a normal animal. T-cells are very long-lived, and there may be no demand for a large number of new cells to be produced in mature animals.

After reaction with antigen, T- and B-cells proliferate and differentiate into memory cells and those which produce the antibody or carry out the cellular responses. This stage in the immune system could be affected by age-related changes in the environment of the cells or by intrinsic changes in the cells themselves. Either the number or the efficiency of the effector cells might be changed. Makinodan and his colleagues (see Makinodan and Adler, 1975) have investigated this part of the immune response by transplanting spleen cells from young or old donor mice into old or young irradiated hosts. They found that 90% of the age-related decline in B-cell responses could be attributed to changes in the cells, only 10% to changes in the environment. The cellular changes did not involve any substantial change in the number of B-cells in the spleen, but there was a reduction in the number of "immunocompetent units", i.e. a reduction in the number of units of interacting T-cells, B-cells and macrophages which are necessary to produce antigen against sheep erythrocytes. Furthermore, the number of antibody-producing progeny cells per immunocompetent unit was 10 times less for old cells than for young.

For the T-cells it has been found that the number in the mouse spleen does not change with age, but when the proliferative response of these cells was measured *in vitro* they showed a marked decrease in their ability to proliferate as the animal became older. B-cells showed a much smaller and slower decline in proliferative ability. This difference in the proliferative capacity of the T- and B-cell populations might result in what Makinodan and Adler call an "unbalanced" immune system, and this could be the cause of some of the deterioration in immune responses.

Williamson and Askonas (1972) have shown that a single clone of antibody-forming cells is not capable of indefinite proliferation *in vivo*. They were able to transfer serially through irradiated host mice a clone of B-cells which could be identified by the antibody which the cells produced. Although high antibody production was maintained through four serial transfers, during subsequent transfer generations it declined, and in the eighth generation the antibody was almost undetectable (figure 6.10). Williamson and Askonas believe that failure to regenerate memory cells was the reason for the decline, and they estimated that the overall proliferative capacity of the clone was not more than 90 divisions.

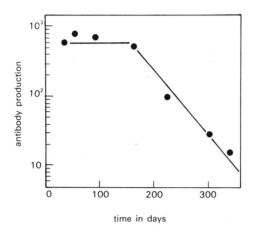

Figure 6.10 Maximum production of antibody in each transplant generation for a single clone of antibody-producing cells (redrawn from Williamson and Askonas, 1972).

6.7 The autoimmune theory of ageing

From the preceding brief description of some of the age-related changes found in the immune system and in immune responses, it should be clear that the deterioration of the immune system is likely to contribute to the increased likelihood of dying from disease in old age. However, some people believe that the decreasing efficiency of the immune system is not simply one of many factors involved in senescence, but rather that senescence is due primarily to deficiencies in this system (Walford, 1969; Burnet, 1974). In particular it has been suggested that ageing can be regarded as what Walford has called "a long-term minor-grade histoincompatibility reaction". Basically what is suggested is that with increasing age the immune system becomes inefficient and there is an increasing chance of the immunocompetent cells reacting against the body's own constituents. Normally lymphocytes are tolerant of "self" antigens. Development of tolerance occurs during the perinatal period, although it is still not clear how it is brought about. The thymus is thought to censor T-cells that could react with "self" antigens and eliminate them or inhibit them from multiplying. Any breakdown of tolerance could lead to the formation of antibodies against self, and it is known that some diseases are due to such autoimmune reactions. For example, in Hashimoto's thyroid disease, antibodies are formed against thyroglobulin; in some forms of haemolytic anaemia, serum factors react against red cells. In addition, many of the characteristic diseases of old age such as amyloidosis, rheumatoid diseases and possibly some malignant diseases, are believed to be associated with autoimmune reactions.

The idea that ageing as well as specific diseases might be due to autoimmune reactions is supported by a lot of indirect evidence. Walford's book provides a detailed discussion of this evidence, so only a few examples will be given here. Possibly the most significant observation is the increased level of autoantibodies found in the blood of normal healthy people as they get older. It has been found that the rheumatoid factor, antibodies for thyroid tissue and gastric parietal cells, and anti-nuclear antibodies all increase with age. Also there is an increased accumulation of lymphocytes and plasma cells in various tissues in old age. It is claimed that the graft-versus-host reaction shows many parallels with normal ageing. The graft-versus-host reaction occurs when lymphocytes are transferred to a recipient animal and react against the host tissues. When this occurs, the animals show changes in the skin and hair, weight loss, increased levels of autoantibodies, amyloidosis, renal changes, etc., all of which tend to resemble changes found during normal ageing.

If many of the changes associated with ageing are due to autoimmune reactions, it must mean that the normal tolerance to self has broken down. There are a number of different ways in which this could happen. Firstly, some of the constituents of the body which are normally shielded from the immune system because they do not come into contact with the lymphocytes might be released as a result of disease or damage, and thus provide a new antigen for which the body has no tolerance. Secondly, as a result of viral infection or mutation, cells might start to produce new antigens which result in them being recognized as "not-self" rather than "self". Thirdly, mutations could occur in the B- or T-cells, which would lead to the production of what Burnet has called a "forbidden clone" reacting against self and not subject to the normal censorship which eliminates or inhibits self-reacting cells.

The merit of the autoimmune theory of ageing is that not only does it suggest a common cause of the variety of age-related changes seen in animals, it also offers an explanation for some of the experimental data which are difficult to reconcile with many of the other theories of ageing. In particular, it can explain the experiments which showed that restricting food intake in youth extends the life-span. Food restriction is known to delay the maturation of immune responses, and might therefore be expected to delay the onset of autoimmune reactions. Furthermore, the experiments in which the life-span of fish was increased by keeping them at low temperatures can also be explained in terms of the autoimmune theory. Low temperatures depress immune responsiveness. It will be recalled that Liu and Walford found that lowering the temperature during the latter half of life had the greatest effect on life-span (Table 5.1). This is exactly what would be expected if autoimmune diseases increase with age, since low temperatures in the second half of life would suppress these autoimmune reactions.

Although the autoimmune hypothesis is attractive, it does have one great drawback as a general hypothesis to explain ageing, namely, that it cannot be applied to non-vertebrate animals. As far as we know, invertebrates lack an immune system comparable with that found in vertebrates.

6.8   Ageing of connective tissues

Connective tissues are made up of cells, fibres such as collagen and elastin, and a ground substance or matrix. This type of tissue is found around and throughout the organs and specialized tissues of the body, but the amount present and its composition varies with the site. Much of bone, skin, tendon and cartilage is connective tissue, but there is very little present in the brain. In the synovial fluid of the joints and the vitreous humour of the eye there is very little fibrous material, whereas the ligaments and tendons are very rich in fibrous elements.

Many age-related changes have been detected in connective tissues, particularly in the composition and properties of the extracellular materials. According to Kohn (1971), most of the ageing changes seen in mammals can be attributed to alterations in these extracellular elements. Since connective tissue is so widespread in distribution, is involved in the transport and exchange of materials between cells and tissues, and serves important structural functions, any deterioration in it is bound to have very profound effects on the physiological capacities of an animal.

It is impossible to review all of the ageing changes found in different types of connective tissues, so the discussion in this section will be largely restricted to a consideration of collagen, one of the extracellular components. This protein has been studied far more intensively than any other constituent of connective tissue. Recently there has been considerable interest in the age-related changes found in the polysaccharide-protein complexes of the ground substance, and it may be that these changes will eventually prove to be more important than those found in the fibrous elements of connective tissues. However, collagen is a major constituent of skin, blood vessels, bone, cartilage and tendons, and it forms over 25% of the total body protein, so it is clearly a very important substance. Moreover, some of the age-related changes found in collagen could also take place in other macromolecules in the body, so collagen ageing can probably serve as a model for ageing in other types of molecules.

Collagen is synthesized by fibroblasts and is probably secreted in a form known as tropocollagen. Each tropocollagen molecule is about 300 nm long, 1.4 nm in diameter, and has a molecular weight of approximately 300,000. It is made up of three polypeptide chains arranged as a triple helix. These polypeptide chains are very rich in the amino acids glycine, proline and hydroxyproline. Since hydroxyproline does not occur in significant amounts in other proteins, it can be used to estimate the collagen content of tissues.

After secretion, the tropocollagen molecules are rapidly incorporated into collagen fibrils. These are formed by side-to-side alignment of molecules. Adjacent molecules overlap each other in a regular way to give a staggered arrangement. Molecules also associate end to end, and in some tissues bundles of fibrils come together to form long thick fibres. The mucopolysaccharides in the matrix of connective tissue are believed to be important in the organization and regulation of fibril formation.

Newly-formed collagen fibrils can be readily extracted from tissue using neutral salt solutions. However, as the collagen matures, covalent cross-linkages occur within and between the molecules, and these make it relatively insoluble. In the adult animal, most collagen seems to be metabolically relatively inert and the turnover rate is low.

A number of different techniques have been used to show that with increasing age of the animal the properties of collagen change. It has been found that measurements of collagen properties are in fact some of the best indicators of age in higher animals. As the animal gets older, the amount of readily soluble collagen decreases. Mature insoluble collagen becomes increasingly difficult to digest with bacterial collagenase. As is shown in figure 6.11, there is an excellent correlation between age and the time taken to digest 50% of the collagen from human-diaphragm tendons. When rat-tail tendon is heated and denatured in neutral salt solution at 58–60°C, it contracts. The maximum weight needed to inhibit this contraction increases as age increases, and the rate of contraction also changes. Similar results have been obtained with tendons from other vertebrates. The tension generated during thermal denaturation of the tendon of a three-year-old cat is similar to that in a rat of the same age, even though the life-spans of the two species are so different. It has also been found that during *in vitro* storage the denaturation tension of collagen increases. Taken together, these pieces of evidence suggest that to some extent the ageing of collagen molecules is an intrinsic process which does not depend on changes in the environment of

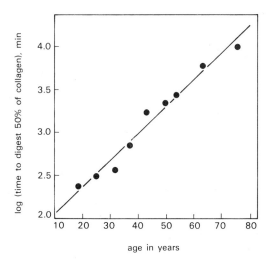

Figure 6.11   Relation between age and the time required to digest 50% of the collagen in human diaphragm tendons (redrawn from Hamlin and Kohn, *Exp. Gerontol.*, **7**, 377, 1972).

the molecules. However, it is known that some conditions which retard animal ageing, e.g. caloric restriction, also retard the changes in collagen. Thus the internal environment can affect the rate at which the molecules age.

The age-related alterations in the properties of collagen molecules are believed to be due either to the formation of more cross-linkages between the molecules, or to the conversion of labile bonds into more stable forms. The reasons for the changes and the nature of the bonds is still not clear. Whatever the causes of the changes, it seems likely that alterations in the structure and quantity of collagen and comparable changes in elastin are responsible for many of the obvious manifestations of ageing in mammals. The loss of flexibility of the skin could be due to increases in the quantity of collagen and elastin, and the increase in the extent of cross-linking. This type of change might also be responsible for the reduction in the vital capacity of the lungs. Changes in the connective-tissue elements in the artery walls make them more rigid and less efficient, and therefore impair the efficiency of the circulatory system.

However, the evidence that cross-linkages in collagen and elastin increase with age has done more than provide an explanation for some of the manifestations of ageing. It has also provided support for the *cross-linkage theory* of ageing. A number of people have speculated that cross-linkages in macromolecules could be the major cause of ageing. Bjorksten (1974) has been one of the major advocates of this theory. He has suggested that, since cross-linking agents such as free radicals are always present, important molecules such as proteins and DNA will inevitably accumulate cross-linkages which will prevent them from functioning normally. There is evidence that nucleoproteins in old animals have a higher temperature stability than those in young animals, and this could be due to increased cross-linking. Cross-linkages in molecules like these could have very far-reaching consequences. They could cause somatic mutations and affect the ability of DNA to replicate. Indeed, if cross-linkages are extensive and the damage that they cause cannot be repaired, they could account for many of the age-related changes in cells and tissues that have been considered in this chapter.

6.9 Conclusions

In this chapter we have considered a wide range of age-related changes in cells and tissues. It is probably true to say that there is no type of cell or tissue that is unaffected by age, although the nature of the changes seen depends on the tissue being studied. For non-renewing tissues we saw that there is some evidence that the long-lived fixed post-mitotic cells decrease in number and that changes within the cells, e.g. lipofuscin accumulation, might affect their ability to function normally. Deterioration in the quantity and quality of the cells in these tissues could therefore cause the functional decline in the whole animal. Equally, though, the changes in the cells of renewing or expanding tissues might be responsible for senescence. The work that we discussed shows that in many tissues there seems to be a decrease in the ability to produce new cells as the animal gets older, and the longevity and properties of the cells produced is not always the same in old and young animals. Even the extracellular materials show definite age-related changes.

As was stated at the beginning of this chapter, it is very difficult to decide which of the many changes that can be observed are important causes of senescence, because it is almost impossible to separate the effects which are intrinsic to the cells themselves from those which depend on the extracellular environment in which the cells are situated. We do not know whether brain cell number decreases because brain cells have only a limited life-span, even in the most favourable conditions, or because their environment deteriorates. We do not know whether the differences in the length of the mitotic cycle in the cells of intestinal crypts are due to changes in the properties of the cells themselves or to changes in the overall physiology of the animal. Although some of the transplantation experiments suggest that ageing changes are intrinsic to the cells, and that dividing cells cannot go on multiplying at a rapid rate indefinitely, the evidence is not very strong. Unfortunately it is almost impossible to demonstrate conclusively by transplantation experiments that cells or tissues have a limited life-expectancy, because failure to grow or divide can always be attributed to technical difficulties.

CHAPTER SEVEN

AGEING OF CELLS AND TISSUES *IN VITRO*

IN ORDER TO UNDERSTAND THE NATURE AND CAUSES OF THE AGEING CHANGES seen in cells and tissues *in vivo*, it is desirable to be able to separate the age-associated changes which are due to the intrinsic deterioration of the cells and tissues themselves from those which are due to the deterioration of the environment in which they are found. One way in which, in theory, this might be achieved is by studying tissues and cells when they are maintained in culture outside the body.

Some of the pioneer studies of ageing *in vitro* were carried out more than 60 years ago by Carrel and his associates (see Hay, 1967). The work of these investigators produced results of considerable interest and importance to gerontologists. They took small pieces of chick embryo tissue and maintained them under sterile conditions in chick serum. After a short period known as the *latent period*, tissue fragments maintained in this way begin to grow because cells migrate out from the tissue and start to divide. Providing the culture medium is replaced frequently, the culture can be maintained for a considerable time.

The first of the important observations that Carrel and his colleagues made using this *in vitro* culture method was that the length of the latent period before cells began to migrate out from the tissue depended on the age of the animal from which the tissue came: the older the animal, the longer the latent period. For example, for spleen explants from 14–16-day-old embryos the latent period was only 2 hours, whereas for adult spleen it was 12 hours.

The second age-dependent relationship found by the early workers was that the serum of old donors was less capable of maintaining growth of the tissues than that from young donors (Table 7.1). They were able to separate two antagonistic factors: a growth-stimulating factor which could be precipitated by bubbling carbon dioxide through the serum, and an inhibitory factor which remained in the supernatant. They found that the concentration of lipids and proteins in the serum increased with age, and that

Table 7.1 Carrel and Ebeling's data on the effect of plasma from chickens of various ages on fibroblast outgrowth (from Hay, 1967).

Donor age	Average number of passages before growth cessation	Average relative rate of outgrowth
6 weeks	20	148
3 months	13	100
3 years	8	51
9 years	2	22

both the lipid and protein components of serum from old chickens were inhibitory. It has subsequently been suggested that, since unsaturated fatty acids are known to have inhibitory and toxic properties, part of the inhibitory effect of old serum might be due to the increased levels of these substances. However, although the observation that the serum of old animals is less capable of supporting growth than the serum of young animals has been confirmed using human tissue and human serum, there seems to have been little further work on this subject. This is surprising since, in spite of the recent advances made in tissue and cell-culture techniques, serum is still essential for the satisfactory culture of most cell types.

Probably the most influential conclusion reached by Carrel was that cells in culture could be maintained and would proliferate indefinitely. He reported the first of the experiments leading to this conclusion in 1912 in a paper entitled "On the permanent life of tissues outside of the organism".

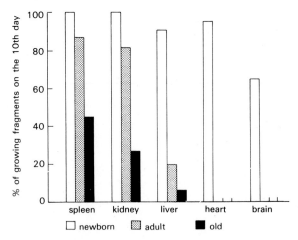

Figure 7.1 The relation between age and the amount of cell migration from explants of rat tissues (redrawn from Michl *et al.*, 1968).

The importance of this conclusion is that, if cells in culture are immortal, but donor age affects both the properties of serum and the rate of growth of tissue fragments in culture, then it seems to suggest that senescence is not an inherent property of cells but is a consequence of the functional interrelationships of cells within tissues and of the tissue environment. Does more recent work support this conclusion?

7.1 Cell migration and donor age

The observation that the latent period before cells begin to migrate from a tissue explant depends on the age of the animal from which it came has been confirmed by a number of investigators using a variety of tissues from several different animals. Figures 7.1 and 7.2 show some of the results obtained by Czech workers who used tissue fragments from newborn, adult and senile rats. Clearly, the length of the latent period depends on the tissue used, as well as the age of the animal from which it came. There was no migration at all from the heart and brain of adult and senile animals. This is presumably associated with the absence of mitotic activity and regenerative ability in these tissues *in situ*.

There could be a number of explanations of the decrease in migratory ability with increase in donor age for the other three tissues. It could be that with increasing donor age the cells themselves are less capable of moving and escaping from the tissue fragment, or that only a proportion of the cells are able to migrate. Alternatively, the increased latent period might be due to changes in the properties of the intercellular matrix which make it more

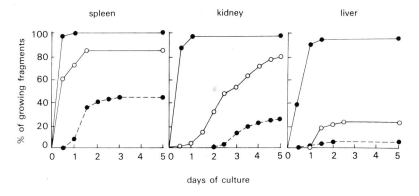

Figure 7.2 The rate of cell migration from explants of tissues from rats of different ages. ●——● newborn, ○——○ adult, ●— — —● old (based on data of Soukupová *et al.*, 1970).

difficult for the cells to escape. The quantitative and qualitative changes in collagen which were described in the last chapter may make cell movement more difficult, or perhaps, as some of the earlier workers suggested, the tissues of old animals contain inhibitors comparable with those found in the serum.

It has been shown that treatment of tissues with proteolytic enzymes reduces the latent period before cell migration. This might be due to their effect in removing chemical and mechanical inhibitory substances from the tissue, but proteolytic enzymes could equally well affect the properties of the cell surface. At present, therefore, it is difficult to know whether changes in the properties of the cells themselves, or changes in the intercellular matrix, or both factors are responsible for the effect of age on the length of the latent period.

7.2   Are cultured cell strains immortal?

Carrel's conclusion that cells in culture are immortal seems to have been generally accepted until about 1960. Although people found that their cultures frequently died out, they were usually prepared to attribute this to the inadequacy of the medium that they were using, or to contamination by microorganisms. Many cell cultures were established in different laboratories and continued to proliferate without any sign of degeneration, so there seemed to be no reason to doubt that cells in culture could be maintained indefinitely. Eventually, however, Carrel's conclusion was challenged, in particular by Hayflick (1965). He came to the conclusion that cultured human diploid cell strains have only a limited life-span *in vitro*.

It is worth considering Hayflick's experiments and observations in some detail, since they have stimulated many other people to carry out experiments in what Hayflick suggests might be called *cytogerontology*. For most experiments, fibroblasts from human embryonic lung tissue were used. Small pieces of tissue were treated with trypsin to separate the cells, and the freed cells were inoculated into culture vessels containing medium. In the culture vessels the cells divided many times until eventually they formed a confluent sheet over the inside of the vessels. When this happens, normal fibroblast cells stop dividing. However, if they are dissociated, resuspended, and inoculated at lower density into fresh medium, then the cells will start dividing again and continue until they again cover the surface of the vessel. Hayflick used a 1:2 subcultivation ratio, i.e. each time that his culture formed a confluent sheet and stopped dividing he used half the cells to initiate a new subculture. He found that by using this technique he could subculture, or "passage", the cells for a number of months. Eventually, however, cell generation time increased, so that cultures needed subculturing less frequently; mitotic activity gradually stopped; cellular debris began to accumulate. In the end, the cultures died out because they could no longer be subcultivated. Replacing the medium or combining together several cultures in order to increase cell density failed to rescue the cultures. What was significant was that this period of culture decline always occurred at approximately the same time – after 50 ± 10 cell doublings. This was true not only for replicate cultures started from the same foetal lung, but also for cultures started from different embryos.

Figure 7.3 shows some of Hayflick's results and figure 7.4 shows his interpretation of the history of the cell cultures. He calls the early growth phase from the time that the cells are released from the tissue to the time when they form the first confluent sheet over the inside of the culture vessel Phase I. The period of active cell division necessitating repeated subculturing is called Phase II, and the period of culture decline is Phase III.

Hayflick realized that there could be a number of reasons for the limited life-span of his cultures. One of the most obvious explanations was that the

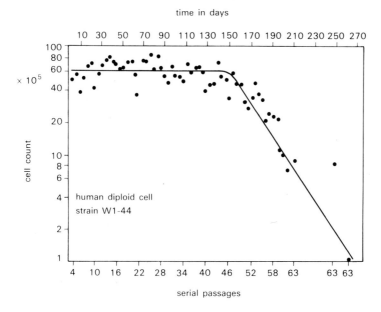

Figure 7.3 Cell counts at each passage of a culture of human foetal lung fibroblasts (redrawn from Hayflick, 1965).

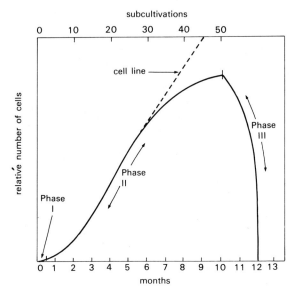

Figure 7.4 Hayflick's representation of cell proliferation *in vitro* (redrawn from Hayflick, 1966).

medium was in some way inadequate. It might, for example, have been deficient in some necessary metabolite, or it might have contained toxic material, or virus or mycoplasma contaminants. Subsequent work suggested that these explanations were unlikely. He supplied many laboratories with samples of his cultures which had been frozen at early passage levels. When they were reconstituted it was found that, in spite of the different culture conditions and media which were used, the cultures always eventually deteriorated. Further evidence suggesting that deficiencies of the medium were not the cause of the failure of the cultures was obtained by mixing cells derived from male embryos which were in Phase III with cells which were in early passage of Phase II and had been obtained from female embryos. If latent microorganisms or medium composition were responsible for the failure of cells in Phase III, it would be expected that Phase II cells would be adversely affected by the presence of Phase III cells, and would therefore die out earlier than in unmixed control cultures. However, the mixed cultures entered Phase III at the same time as the unmixed control cultures. By examining the chromosomes of the cells in the mixed cultures it was shown that the "old" male cells were rapidly lost, and that when the culture reached Phase III only female cells were present. Since the "old" male cells had no detectable effect on the "young" female cells or *vice versa*, it is unlikely that toxic substances or contaminant microorganisms were the cause of the Phase III decline of cultures.

Another possibility considered by Hayflick was that the cause of culture decline was the depletion of some cellular pool of essential metabolites which was present in the primary cell population but could not be synthesized during *in vitro* cultivation. Simple arithmetic suggested that this was unlikely. Since the cultures died after about 50 cell doublings, the original pool of this essential metabolite must have been large enough to supply at least one molecule to each of the daughter cells at the fiftieth passage. The number of daughter cells produced by a cell after 50 divisions is approximately 10^{15}, so each of the original cells must have contained 10^{15} molecules of the hypothetical essential metabolite. Even if the "essential metabolite" was a hydrogen molecule, the weight of 10^{15} molecules would be 3.3×10^{-9}g, which is greater than the weight of the cell (2×10^{-9}g). Although these calculations rule out the possibility that culture decline is due to gradual depletion of molecules of a necessary metabolite which cells are unable to synthesize *in vitro*, they do not of course exclude the possibility that, although the cells are able to synthesize all necessary metabolites, they cannot do so at a rate great enough to keep them at an adequate level.

As a result of these and other experiments and arguments, Hayflick concluded that the most likely explanation of his results was that cells *in vitro* are capable of going through only a limited number of cell doublings, and that this is an innate property of the cells, not a consequence of inadequate culture conditions. Cell cultures are not immortal as Carrel suggested. If this is so, then how was Carrel able to maintain embryonic chick fibroblasts in culture for 34 years, and why have other workers been able to maintain so many mammalian cell populations in culture for long periods?

No one has been able to repeat Carrel's original experiment with chick embryo fibroblasts. Hayflick suggested that the method of preparation of the chick embryo extract which Carrel used as a source of nutrients for his cultures was such that new embryonic cells may have been inadvertently added to the cultures every time that nutrient was provided.

The explanation which Hayflick suggested for the fact that apparently immortal cell cultures do exist and are maintained and subcultured in many laboratories is of rather more importance. He suggested that only abnormal cells could be cultured indefinitely; the cells in immortal cultures are not normal, but have all the properties of cancer cells. They differ from the cells in the cultures that he used in that they do not have the normal diploid chromosome number of the animal from which the tissue came, but are heteroploid. Histologically they do not look like normal cells. They form tumour masses when inoculated into suitable hosts. Hayflick therefore made a distinction between *cell lines* which will multiply indefinitely in culture, and *cell strains* which have only a limited *in vitro* life, and suggested that cell lines and cell strains bear the same relationship to each other as the relationship between transplantable tumours and normal tissue:

in vitro	cell line	cell strain
karyotype	heteroploid	diploid
histological appearance	cancer cells	normal
growth potential	infinite	finite
in vivo	transplantable tumour	normal somatic tissue

Many immortal cell lines are known to have been derived from cancer tissue. For example, HeLa cells came from cervical cancer tissue. However, many other cell lines originated with cells from apparently normal tissue. In culture, cell strains can spontaneously alter to become cell lines at any time. The chances of this occurring depend on the animal from which the cells came. Mouse and rat cell strains are very likely to convert spontaneously to cell lines, whereas it is rather unusual for human or chick-cell strains to alter.

If the conclusion that there is a fundamental difference between normal cells with a limited *in vitro* life-span and cell lines with an unlimited life-span *in vitro* is correct, then it has the important implication that senescence is a property of the cells themselves, but that cells are capable of escaping from the inevitability of senescence. In practical terms, the difference between cell strains and lines means that comparisons of the two types of culture might provide valuable information about the nature and causes of senescence and of cancer.

Hayflick's observations have been confirmed by many people, but unfortunately there are experimental results which suggest that the differences between cell lines and cell strains may not be quite as simple and clear-cut as was originally thought. For example, a number of people have been able to maintain some cell cultures for very long periods without any apparent change in the karyotype of the cells occurring. Puck *et al.* (1966) kept a clone of rabbit cells in culture for over 500 generations and found that at the end of this period the chromosome number was normal. However, one chromosome was morphologically different, and it is possible that this chromosome abnormality was associated with the immortality of the culture. It may be that the recent advances in karyotype analysis will reveal other as yet undetected changes in the apparently normal karyotypes of other immortal cell populations.

Hay (1970) and a number of other workers believe that even if cell strains do have a limited life-span, this life-span is related to the time spent in culture rather than to the number of cell doublings that the strain has been through. One of the experiments which led to this conclusion involved keeping cultures stationary, i.e. without cell division, by overlaying the confluent sheet of cells with agar. Under these conditions cells remain alive, since nutrients can reach them through the agar, but there is very little room for cell division to occur. When the agar is removed and the cells are resuspended, active cell division begins again. It was found that the total number of divisions that the cells went through before the onset of Phase III degeneration was inversely proportional to the period that they had spent under the agar, but the total calendar time for which the cultures could be maintained was the same as for cultures which had never been subjected to the agar treatment. This may mean that it is the time that the cells are metabolically active rather than the number of cell divisions that determines the culture life-span. The fact that cultures grown at 40°C rather than the usual 37°C used for mammalian cultures also undergo fewer doublings before Phase III degeneration tends to support the suggestion that metabolic activity may be more important than the number of doublings.

Another observation which slightly complicates the simple picture that Hayflick presented is that addition of some substances to the culture medium will prolong the life-span of the cultures. Addition of hydrocortisone or vitamin E will increase the number of doublings before Phase III occurs, and the addition of "feeder" cells (i.e. irradiated cells which cannot themselves divide but which are capable of metabolic activity) has been reported to increase the survival of cell strains. For these reasons it has been suggested that senescence may be a consequence of culture conditions rather than a fundamental property of the cells themselves, and that further refinements of culture techniques may result in indefinite survival. Nevertheless, the evidence at present available is that, although additives may increase the survival of fibroblast cell strains, ultimately division does slow down, and the cultures can no longer be subcultivated.

7.3 The relation between ageing of cells *in vitro* and ageing *in vivo*

If cells are capable of only a limited number of cell divisions, then it would be predicted that cell strains started with material from adult tissues would have a shorter life-span than those which are started from foetal tissue, since the cells would have gone through a number of divisions *in situ* during the development of the adult. Hayflick showed that this was indeed so: cells derived from adult lung tissue reached Phase III after only about 20 doublings, whereas foetal lung cells went through 50 + 10 doublings. These results have been confirmed and extended by Martin *et al.* (1970) who have shown that there is a clear inverse correlation between the age of the donor and the doubling potential of skin fibroblasts (figure 7.5). On the average, the doubling potential is reduced by 0.2 for every year of age of the donor. Even more interesting is the observation that skin fibroblasts from people with Werner's syndrome (a form of inherited premature senescence which was described in chapter 4) have a greatly reduced doubling potential. It appears, therefore, that there is a relation between the life-span of cells in culture and the expectation of life of the donor.

Another interesting observation made by Martin *et al.* was that the number of fibroblast cell doublings which occurred before the onset of Phase III depended on the tissue from which the cells came. Fibroblasts from the skin of young people always went through more than 27 doublings, whereas those from skeletal muscle or bone marrow spicules rarely ap-

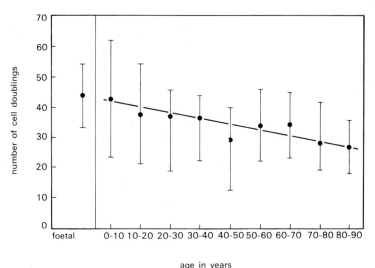

Figure 7.5   The number of cell doublings before culture death for skin fibroblasts from donors of different ages. The circles give the mean and the bars indicate the range of doublings found for each age group (modified after Martin *et al.*, 1970).

Table 7.2 The life-span of cultured normal human and animal fibroblasts (from Hayflick, 1975).

Species	Range of population doublings	Maximum life-span (years
Galapagos tortoise	90 – 125	175 (?)
Man	40 – 60	110
Mink	30 – 34	10
Chicken	15 – 35	30
Mouse	14 – 28	3.5

proached such a high value. It was suggested that these differences in doubling potential *in vitro* probably reflect differences in the previous *in vivo* history of the cell lineage.

Recently Hayflick (1975) has collected together data on the doubling potential of embryonic fibroblasts from different species. Although at present the amount of data is small, and there are reports that cell cultures from rats and other short-lived species may continue indefinitely, there is some suggestion in Table 7.2 that the correlation between donor's expectation of life and the doubling potential of the cells also holds for different species.

In the last chapter it was pointed out that, although there are great technical problems involved in *in vivo* transplantation experiments and the results obtained have not always been entirely consistent, most of the evidence that is available does suggest that normal cells and tissues have only a limited survival time *in vivo*, whereas tumour cells and tissues can be transferred indefinitely. In other words, the differences found *in vitro* parallel those found in *in vivo* experiments. It seems reasonable, therefore, to conclude that the finite lifetime of cell cultures is in some way related to ageing *in vivo*.

7.4 The multiplication of cells *in vivo*

If cells do have only a limited doubling potential, how is it that cell replacement in the epidermis, bone marrow and intestinal mucosa can go on indefinitely? It has been estimated that there are 28×10^{12} erythrocytes in circulation in a 70-kg man. The average life-span of an erythrocyte is about 120 days. This means that $\frac{1}{120}$ of the total number of erythrocytes are destroyed and replaced daily. Therefore, $\frac{1}{120} \times 28 \times 10^{12}$, approximately 2.3×10^{11}, cells are replaced every day. Assuming that this rate is constant throughout life, a person living for a hundred years would have to produce about 10^{16} red blood cells, an extremely large number. The germinative layer of the epidermis is replaced every 4–8 days. This means that it is replaced about 5000 times in a life-span of 100 years.

At first sight these figures make it seem unlikely that cells *in vivo* can be limited to only 50 divisions. However, closer examination shows that even if cells *in vivo* do have a limited capacity for replication, 50 or so cell doublings might be more than sufficient to provide for all the necessary cell replacement in a man's life-span. The critical question is how cell replacement takes place.

Two extreme models for cell replacement can be considered (Kay, 1965). These are illustrated in figure 7.6 A and B. In the first, the *tangential* model, each stem cell divides and one daughter cell goes on to differentiate, while the other becomes the new stem cell which in turn produces one cell which will differentiate and one which becomes a stem cell, and so on. If cells were

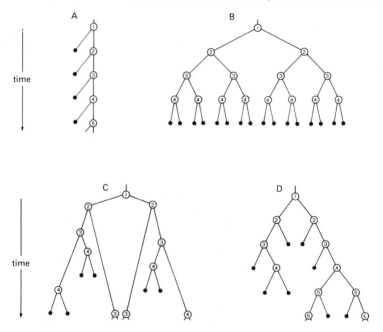

Figure 7.6 Some possible models for cell replacement. The solid circles represent a differentiating cell incapable of further division; open circles are stem cells.
Diagram A shows simple tangential division: four divisions give four differentiated cells and the stem cell remains.
B shows simple logarithmic division: cells divide symmetrically four times and then all differentiate.
C shows asynchronous logarithmic division with differentiation after the fourth division.
D shows a pattern intermediate between the tangential and logarithmic patterns.

limited to only 50 divisions, then only 50 differentiated cells would be produced if this type of cell division occurred. A very large initial stem-cell population would be required to maintain epidermis or red-cell numbers if this was the method of replacement.

The second extreme method of cell replacement would not demand a large primary stem-cell population, but nevertheless it does not seem to be a very likely model for the *in vivo* situation. According to this *logarithmic* model, each stem cell divides to form two daughter cells, each of which will divide again to give two daughter cells, and so on. After a number of divisions, all daughter cells differentiate. If 50 cell divisions occurred before differentiation, then a total of 2^{50} or approximately 10^{15} cells would be produced by a single primary stem-cell. This would probably be enough to provide almost all the red cells needed in the entire life-span of a long-lived man! As it is shown in figure 7.6B, this model would result in all cells differentiating at the same time. This might be appropriate for growth, but not for cell replacement. If, however, the division of daughter cells is asynchronous (as is shown in figure 7.6C) new cells could be provided gradually over a period, even though all cells differentiated after a fixed number of divisions.

Figure 7.6D shows a pattern intermediate between the tangential and logarithmic models which also allows for gradual cell replacement. A stem cell may divide to produce daughter cells, both of which may differentiate, or one of which may differentiate, or both of which may remain as stem cells capable of further division. The decision as to which cells differentiate and which remain as stem cells capable of further division does not depend on the number of divisions needed to produce the cell; *in vivo* it might depend on the spatial arrangements of the different cell lineages. With this type of cell replacement, the number of cells produced from each primary stem-cell after 50 doublings might be very large, although not as large as for the purely logarithmic model.

The four models which have been described are not the only ones which are possible. All are unrealistically simple, since there may be a series of stages between a primary stem-cell and a differentiated end-cell incapable of further division. Nevertheless, the models do serve to show that in theory a limit of 50 divisions need not impose any limitation on the life-span of individual animals due to exhaustion of the capacity to replace cells. Whether or not it does in practice will be decided only when we know much more about cell lineages *in vivo* than we do at present, and when it is definitely established whether or not cells *in vivo* do have a limited proliferative capacity.

7.5   Changes which accompany ageing of cell strains

So far we have been considering the longevity of cell cultures rather than ageing in these cultures. Longevity has been taken as the period between the initiation of the culture and the time when subcultivation is no longer possible. Hayflick's work suggests that the appropriate scale for measuring longevity is the number of cell doublings, whereas Hay and others believe that the time for which cells are metabolically active is also important – calendar time would therefore be a more suitable scale to use. Whichever scale is appropriate, it is important to know the nature of the changes which occur in the cells during the life-span of the culture. In what ways do early passage cells differ from late passage cells? Is there any correlation between the age-dependent changes seen in cells *in vivo* and the cellular changes *in vitro*?

Since the original reports of the limited *in vitro* life-span of cell strains, numerous studies of the morphology, ultrastructure and biochemistry of the cells in culture have been made (see Cristofalo, 1972). Diploid cell strains can be transformed by viruses to cell lines capable of indefinite proliferation. The comparison of sister cell lines and cell strains is therefore possible. These studies are important, not only because of their possible relevance to understanding ageing, but also because they may throw light on the nature and causes of the differences between normal and cancer cells.

As cell strains age, cell size increases and becomes more variable. There tends to be a decrease in the number of cells per unit area when the cells become confluent at the end of each passage. The increase in cell size does not seem to be associated with an increase in polyploidy as judged by the average DNA content per cell, or by chromosome counts made during mitosis. It has been found, however, that chromosome aberrations are more common in cells from late passages.

Ultrastructural studies have shown that the nuclei of cells from late passages are less regular in shape than those of early passage cells. Although there are no changes in the number of mitochondria with passage level, there is an increase in the proportion with incomplete transverse cristae. The endoplasmic reticulum has more ribosome-free segments in cells from older cultures. By far the most striking change that is seen in the cells is a gradual increase in the number of lysosomes and residual bodies with increase in passage number. Residual bodies are thought to be associated with previous lysosomal activity and autophagocytosis. The increased prominence of the Golgi apparatus in late passage cells is also probably connected with previous increased lysosome formation and activity. What is not clear is whether or not the increase in lysosomes and residual bodies is directly related to the number of cell doublings. There is some evidence that cells from early passages which are stopped from dividing by not sub-culturing them when they form confluent sheets also accumulate residual bodies. This suggests that increase in residual bodies may be due to the lowered mitotic activity found with increased passage level, rather than to the number of cell doublings. Cell division presumably dilutes residual bodies.

Biochemical differences between Phase-II and Phase-III cells have been found. Lipid and RNA content per cell increase with passage number and, although the evidence is not entirely consistent, late-passage fibroblasts seem to utilize more glucose per cell. RNA and protein synthesis decrease with culture age. As might be expected from the ultrastructural studies, lysosomal enzyme levels are higher in late-passage cells. Some of the most fascinating results obtained from biochemical investigations of diploid human cell strains are those which suggest that there is a decline in the quality rather than quantity of the enzymes produced in cells from old cultures. These results will be discussed fully in the next chapter, when we consider some of the molecular mechanisms which have been proposed as explanations of senescence.

The decline in growth capacity of cells in Phase III is the most striking characteristic of fibroblast cell strains. There are several factors contributing to the decline in growth. Firstly, there is an increase in the proportion of cells which do not divide at all. Even in young cultures it has been shown by analysing clones derived from single cells that many cells have a low doubling potential. With increasing passage level, this proportion increases. Secondly, in those cells which are still capable of division, it has been found that the generation time is longer. There is evidence that both the G_1 and G_2 stages of the mitotic cycle are longer. Recently it has been shown that the rate of DNA replication is slower in senescent cells. These results suggest that the whole of the mitotic cycle is stretched out in cells from old cultures.

From the preceding brief description of some of the changes which occur in ageing cell strains *in vitro*, it will be realized that many of the changes at least superficially seem to resemble those found *in vivo*. Increased variability in cell size, slowing down of the rate of cell division, increased lysosomal enzyme activity, and accumulation of lysosome end-products have all been found both *in vivo* and *in vitro*.

7.6   Are *in vitro* studies important?

There is agreement that a limited life-span is a general, if not universal, characteristic of normal diploid fibroblast cells when they are kept in culture conditions which will maintain cancer cell lines indefinitely. However, it is by no means generally accepted that this characteristic has any relevance to the senescence of whole animals. It is worth while considering briefly a few of the reasons why some people believe that the study of cell strains in culture may be unimportant in understanding ageing.

Firstly, as we have already discussed, it can be argued that a limit to only about 50 divisions per cell lineage would not necessarily be of any importance to the animal, since 50 divisions can probably provide all the cells needed for replacement in- an animal's life-span. This does not, however, mean that the limited life-span of cultures is irrelevant. The inability to continue active cell division is only a convenient end-point to use in measuring the longevity of cultures. The events which ultimately result in this inability to divide may have been initiated many cell generations prior to the cessation of cell division. It is known that *in vitro* one of the first signs of ageing is a decline in the rate of protein synthesis. It is not unreasonable to assume that this type of change *in vivo* would impair the general functioning of cells, so that they would deteriorate long before they lost the ability to divide. If this is so, then even if animals are able to replace cells throughout their life-span, new cells would be less efficient than their predecessors, and this would lead to an age-related decline in the functioning of the whole animal. If this argument is correct, studies of cell cultures might provide extremely useful information relevant to ageing *in vivo*.

A second reason for suggesting that studies of ageing of cells *in vitro* are unlikely to contribute much to understanding ageing of whole animals is that most cells cannot be maintained *in vitro* at all. A number of different tissues have been used to initiate cell cultures, but in the end the cells which are maintained are usually "fibroblasts". Other cell types are presumably less capable of proliferation in normal culture conditions. Cell culture fibroblasts may not be typical of all cell types, and studying only one or a few cell types in culture could provide a biased or incorrect picture of general cell ageing. It is well known that tissue and organ survival and function *in vivo* involve the interaction of a number of different types of cell. The inability to culture many cells and the ultimate failure of diploid fibroblast cultures may simply be due to the absence of the other cells which are necessary for normal maintenance and survival. Franks (1970) has given an example from his own experimental work which illustrates this point. He found that normal human prostate epithelium fails to survive in culture when it is separated from the stroma. On the other hand, prostate organ cultures and primary cultures from undissociated tissue can be maintained *in vitro* quite well. The fact that "feeder" cells prolong the life-spans of fibroblast cultures also suggests that cell interrelations are important.

To many people, a limited potential for cell division seems unlikely, because it is difficult to see how cells can "count" the number of divisions. This is certainly a problem, but Holliday (1975) has discussed two possible molecular mechanisms by which cells could count mitoses. Furthermore, there are reasons for thinking that some cells can do this *in vivo*. For example, in the ovaries of *D. melanogaster* a stem-line oogonium divides tangentially to produce a further stem-line oogonium and a cystoblast cell. The latter then goes through four mitotic divisions to produce 16 cystocyte cells, one of which becomes the oocyte and 15 of which differentiate into nurse cells which support the growth of the egg. The capacity to go through four mitotic divisions seems to be a genetically programmed property of the cystocyte cells themselves, rather than a consequence of the organization of the gonad. Mutations are known which remove the limitation to four divisions. In the male there is a similar situation – the secondary spermatogonia undergo four mitotic divisions to produce 16 primary spermatocytes, each of which divides meiotically so that bundles of 64 differentiating spermatozoa are produced. Related species have bundles of 128 spermatozoa. Again this suggests an innate limited capacity for cell division. If some cells *in vivo* are able to "count" mitoses, then there is no justification for thinking that others cannot, even though we do not know exactly how they do it.

Dykhuizen (1974) has speculated that a limited capacity for cell division may be of positive selective advantage *in vivo*. He argues that if a cell gets out of place in the body, it may not be subjected to the normal tissue controls inhibiting division. An innate limited capacity for cell division could stop cells which have escaped from normal tissue control from dividing indefinitely. Natural selection would favour mechanisms limiting cell division, since indefinite growth of "escaped" cells would kill the animal. The number of divisions favoured by selection would be the result of a balance between selection for a high division potential to allow for normal cell replacement, and selection for a restricted number of divisions to control abnormal growths. Dykhuizen suggests that benign tumours and atherosclerotic plaques may be caused by cells which have escaped from their normal tissue and are restricted in growth because of their limited doubling potential. This idea that a limited capacity for cell division is a positive selective advantage is certainly interesting, although the supporting evidence is not at present very substantial. Dykhuizen does, however, suggest ways in which supporting evidence might be obtained.

It is clear from the preceding discussion that at present there is a lack of agreement about the significance and importance to gerontology of the work on survival times of cell strains in culture. At one extreme are the people who believe that what is being studied is an artefact due to inadequacies of the culture medium or to the inappropriateness of studying isolated cell types. At the other extreme are those who believe that what is being studied is a fundamental property of cells, and that cell strains *in vitro* are ideal model systems for studying ageing. What is undoubtedly true is that the finding that cell strains have a limited life-span *in vitro* has initiated a large amount of interesting experimental work and has led to some stimulating ideas about cell survival and ageing *in vivo*.

CHAPTER EIGHT

MOLECULAR MECHANISMS OF AGEING

IN THE PRECEDING CHAPTERS WE HAVE MENTIONED SOME OF THE BIOCHEMICAL differences between old and young animals, and between old and young cells. We have also considered a number of theories of ageing, such as the somatic-mutation theory and cross-linkage theory, which suggest that declining vigour in old age is a consequence of various types of molecular change. In this chapter we shall first look at some of the other theories which relate age-associated deterioration to random changes in various macromolecules, and then consider theories which suggest that senescence is a consequence of the molecular events which bring about differentiation and development.

8.1 The free-radical hypothesis

Free radicals are chemical species which contain an unpaired electron in an outer orbital. This unpaired electron makes them very reactive. They are produced as transient intermediates in the course of normal metabolism, as for example in the oxidative processes found in mitochondria; but it has been suggested that some of these free radicals produced in metabolic reactions, as well as those of random spontaneous origin, may contribute to ageing processes. Since free radicals may attack important molecules such as DNA, proteins and lipids, and since they also tend to be self-propagating, they are capable of generating considerable damage.

The hypothesis that ageing changes are the result of accumulated free-radical damage was based in part on the observation that some types of radiation injury resemble the changes seen in natural ageing. Much of the damage caused by ionizing radiation is thought to be initiated by the ionization of water, and the formation and subsequent reactions of OH·, OOH· and H· radicals. These radicals can react with organic molecules, and lead to polymerization and peroxidation. Although both the damage caused by radiation and that accumulating during natural ageing may be initiated by free-radical attack, there is no reason to expect the pathologies to be exactly the same, because the distribution of free radicals produced by irradiation will be different from that of free radicals produced in non-irradiated cells.

Free radicals can attack proteins and DNA, and may lead to cross-linkages within or between these molecules. However, it seems to be generally agreed that intracellular membranes are likely to be particularly susceptible to free-radical damage because they are so rich in unsaturated fatty acids. Free-radical action induces peroxidation of unsaturated fatty acids, and this could affect the functioning of the membranes. For example, reactions producing cross-linking or lipid-chain splitting in mitochondrial membranes could render mitochondria non-functional. The single membranes of lysosomes might, if damaged, break down or become leaky, so that hydrolytic enzymes are released; these enzymes might in turn cause damage to other cytoplasmic and nuclear components, and eventually to the extracellular material. Peroxidation reactions in membrane lipids might affect transport processes across cell and organelle membranes, and thus affect cell functioning.

According to Gordon (1974), many of the changes that lipid peroxidation injury would be expected to produce are in fact found in old animals. For example, in blowflies the flight-muscle mitochondria show ultrastructural changes with age, and they also have a decreased ability to respire normally. The accumulation of lipofuscin pigment in cells is an excellent indicator of age, and some people believe that this substance is the end-product formed when membranes are damaged and cannot be completely metabolized by the cells. It is worth noting that one of the richest deposits of lipofuscin is in the rodent testis, which also has a very high unsaturated lipid content. Furthermore, vitamin E deficiency and hyperoxia both increase the rate of lipofuscin accumulation, and they are also known to increase free-radical action on unsaturated lipids. Conversely, animals fed on high vitamin E diets accumulate lipofuscin more slowly.

If ageing changes are caused by free-radical damage to membranes and other cellular components, substances which scavenge free radicals or stabilize cell membranes would be expected to prolong the life-span of cells and animals. There is some evidence which suggests that they do. Vitamin E has been added to the diet of *Drosophila* and mice, and in some cases it has been found to produce an increase in life-span. Some artificial antioxidants have also been found to have longevity enhancing effects, although the results of this type of experiment have not been entirely consistent, and they can often be interpreted in other ways, e.g. the antioxidants may affect longevity because they affect food intake by the animals.

There is little doubt that the life-span of fibroblast cultures can be increased dramatically by the addition of vitamin E or hydrocortisone, which is also a membrane stabilizer. Packer and Smith (1974) found that addition of vitamin E at the 45th generation of a culture which normally died out after 65 population doublings increased its life-span to over 100 doublings without affecting its karyotype. Furthermore, tests for the presence of the decomposition products of unsaturated fatty acids showed that their level was much lower in vitamin-E-treated cultures. The effects of visible light and increased oxygen tension (both of which increase free-radical production and have life-shortening effects on cells in culture) were also reduced by the addition of vitamin E. Thus these experiments do suggest that membrane damage may be involved in the failure of fibroblast cultures, and therefore that free-radical attack may be one of the causes of cellular ageing changes.

8.2 The error catastrophe hypothesis

In 1963 Orgel suggested that a progressive decrease in the accuracy of protein synthesis might be one of the factors contributing to the age-related deterioration of cells. He pointed out that metabolic errors are inevitable and, although most of them are unlikely to be important, some might lead to further errors and eventually result in the cell containing so many faulty molecules that it is no longer able to function normally.

Information about proteins is coded in DNA in the nucleus. Protein synthesis involves the transcription and translation of this information. For any particular protein, the base sequences in DNA which code for the polypeptide chains are first transcribed into messenger RNA. At the ribosomes in the cytoplasm, mRNA is translated into the sequences of amino acids which make up the polypeptide chains.

DNA also contains the information for the production of ribosomal RNAs and transfer RNAs. Ribosomal RNAs are important components of ribosomes, and transfer RNAs are adaptor molecules which transport specific amino acids to the ribosomes and place them in the appropriate positions in the polypeptide chain dictated by mRNA.

Some of the proteins which are translated at ribosomes are themselves part of the translation machinery, e.g. ribosomal proteins, the RNA polymerase involved in transcription, and the aminoacyl-tRNA synthetase molecules which activate amino acids and attach them to their appropriate tRNA molecules. It is these proteins which Orgel suggested might be important in ageing.

Consider a situation in which a fault occurs and an incorrect amino acid is inserted into a polypeptide chain. In many cases this will be unimportant, because the resulting protein will still be able to function normally. Occasionally, however, an incorrect amino acid will result in the protein having an impaired function. The consequences to the cell of such defective protein molecules may be negligible or disastrous, depending on the type of protein involved. If the faulty protein is one which is involved in short-lived physical structures, or it is an enzyme concerned with intermediary metabolism, it is unlikely to affect cell function seriously. After all, it will be only one among many normal protein molecules, and it will probably be degraded soon after it is formed. Its existence will have no long-term consequences. If, however, the faulty protein molecule is one which is involved in the transcription and translation machinery of the cell, its presence could have very serious secondary effects. For example, a defective RNA polymerase molecule could cause mistranscription of the DNA message and hence induce further errors; a mistake in a tRNA synthetase molecule could lead to incorrect amino acids being inserted into growing polypeptide chains. Since the enzymes involved in transcription and translation will play a part in the formation of many new protein molecules, and since some of these new protein molecules may themselves be part of the transcription and translation machinery, the original defective protein might lead to what Orgel called "an error catastrophe". Such an error catastrophe might be responsible for the deterioration and death of a cell.

If Orgel's hypothesis is correct, then it leads to at least three testable predictions. The first is that the degenerative changes accompanying ageing should be primarily of cytoplasmic rather than nuclear origin. The second is that abnormal proteins should be detectable in old cells and animals. The third prediction is that any natural or artificially induced increase in the frequency of errors in protein synthesis should lead to premature senescence. We shall consider each of these predictions in turn.

Evidence that the cytoplasm rather than the nucleus is the site of degenerative changes has come from work with Protozoa, fungi and human cells. In *Amoeba*, cultures may be either immortal or "spanned" (chapter 4). Spanned cultures are produced by environmental manipulation and have only a limited life-span. It has been shown that spanned amoebae cannot be changed to the immortal state either by putting a normal nucleus into a spanned cytoplasm, or by putting a spanned nucleus into a normal cytoplasm. Thus both nuclear and cytoplasmic factors seem to be associated with spanning. However, it has also been shown that injecting cytoplasm from spanned amoebae into normal amoebae causes some of the latter to become spanned. In other words, as would be expected if defective protein synthesis machinery was partially responsible for spanning, spanned cytoplasm can transfer its characteristics to a normal cell.

Results obtained with the fungus *Podospora* tend to confirm this observation. If this fungus is prevented from reproducing sexually, it will continue to grow steadily for some time but then, rather suddenly, growth rate declines, a brown pigment is produced, morphological changes occur, and the culture dies. It has been shown by appropriate crosses that this degeneration is caused by a cytoplasmic factor, i.e. it is inherited with the cytoplasm, not with the nucleus. Also, fusion of senescent and non-senescent mycelia results in the senescent mycelium "infecting" the normal one and causing it to die prematurely.

The experimental results obtained with human cells in culture have been less consistent in supporting the idea that cytoplasmic factors control senescence. By using Sendai virus it is possible to cause fibroblasts to fuse and form multinucleate cells. When old and young cells were fused, it was found that DNA synthesis in the young nuclei was inhibited. This suggests, although it does not prove, that old cytoplasm may have affected the young nuclei adversely. However, experiments carried out by Wright and Hayflick (1975) led to a rather different conclusion about the importance of the cytoplasm. They were able to enucleate human cells and fuse the resulting anucleate cytoplasm with whole cells of a different age to give *heteroplasmons*. Young cytoplasm (i.e. from cells in early Phase II) could not rejuvenate old cells (from late Phase II or Phase III). Furthermore, some of the heteroplasmons formed from old cytoplasm and young cells grew just as well as controls of young cytoplasm and young cells. These results suggest that cell senescence is not due to cytoplasmic events, because old cytoplasm did not age young cells. However, at present the amount of data from this type of experiment is small, and as Wright and Hayflick admit, the elaborate procedure which is necessary to produce heteroplasmons means that their conclusion that the control of senescence is nuclear rather than cytoplasmic can only be regarded as tentative.

The second prediction of Orgel's hypothesis is that with increasing age there should be an increase in the amount of defective protein. Direct evidence for old cells containing higher levels of proteins with incorrect amino acids is not available, because detecting these errors is technically very difficult. Nevertheless, it has been shown that with advancing age tissues and cells contain defective enzymes which could have been produced by mistranslation.

It is known that random amino-acid substitutions frequently make enzymes more susceptible to heat denaturation. Holliday and Tarrant (1972)

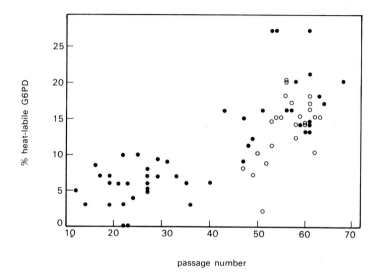

Figure 8.1 Changes in the amount of heat-labile enzyme in human fibroblast cultures. Closed circles are measurements with assorted cell lines of different ages; open circles are successive measurements on a single cell line (redrawn from Holliday and Tarrant, 1972).

therefore measured the size of the heat-labile fraction for the enzymes glucose-6-phosphate dehydrogenase (G6PD) and 6-phosphogluconate dehydrogenase (6PGD) extracted from fibroblast cells from cultures of different ages. Some of their results are shown in figure 8.1. Young cells had only about 5% of heat-labile enzyme but, after passage 40, the amount increased rapidly and reached 27% in some late-passage cells. Both of the enzymes studied behaved in a similar way.

Holliday and Tarrant were also able to show that the heat-labile fraction of enzyme found in old cells had an altered substrate specificity. That is to say, it reacted with an analogue substrate with a higher efficiency than normal enzyme. Since some amino-acid substitutions are known to alter substrate specificity, this is further evidence that some of the enzyme in old cells may contain incorrect amino acids as a result of mistranslation.

Another technique which has been used to assess the proportion of defective enzyme in ageing cells and tissues involves a comparison between the amount of enzyme measured by an immunological technique and that measured by an enzymatic technique. The immunological technique measures the antigenic activity of the protein (the amount of cross-reacting material or CRM), whereas the enzymatic technique measures its catalytic activity. Therefore, if the amount of antigenic activity for a given enzymatic activity increases with age, it implies that some of the protein molecules in old cells are catalytically inactive. By using this technique it has been shown that there is an age-associated increase in the proportion of inactive lactic dehydrogenase in human fibroblasts, isocitrate lyase in the nematode *Turbatrix aceti*, and aldolase in mice livers. Thus for a number of species there is evidence that ageing is accompanied by an increasing amount of defective protein.

There is also some evidence that the longevity differences within a species may be associated with different rates of accumulation of defective enzyme. Fibroblasts from the skin of people with Werner's syndrome have a reduced doubling potential in culture. They also show an increased amount of heat-labile enzyme at an early passage level (Table 8.1). Therefore this type of genetically determined premature senescence is accompanied by a relatively early increase in the level of defective protein molecules. It has been suggested that the mutation involved here may be in a gene coding for part of the machinery of protein synthesis.

Before leaving the subject of defective enzymes, it is as well to point out that it is not a prediction of the error catastrophe hypothesis that there should be a decline in the amount of enzyme activity in tissues of old

Table 8.1 Amount of heat-labile G6PD in Werner's syndrome fibroblasts compared with that in fibroblasts from other sources (data from Holliday *et al*, 1974).

Source of fibroblasts	Passage number	% heat-labile enzyme
Skin of a 46-year-old man suffering from Werner's syndrome	7	21
	9	23
	9	22
	11	22
	11	21
Skin of a normal 54-year-old man	11	9
	25	8
	27	6
Skin of a normal 40-year-old woman	8	4
Skin of a normal 25-year-old man	22	4
Male foetal lung	10 – 40	range 0 – 10 mean 5.8
	53 – 68 (senescent)	range 10 – 27 mean 16.7

animals. If it was, then the hypothesis would have to be rejected, because there is ample evidence to show that, although some enzyme activity is lower in some tissues of old animals, for other enzymes or tissues the level of activity may remain constant throughout life or even increase. The Orgel hypothesis is not concerned with the level of enzyme activity *per se* – this will be controlled by the feedback mechanisms of the cells. It merely predicts that, for a given level of enzyme activity, more enzyme molecules may be needed as age increases, because an increasing proportion of them will be defective.

The third prediction of Orgel's hypothesis, namely that increasing the protein error frequency should increase the rate of ageing and shorten the life-span, was in fact the first to be studied experimentally. Orgel suggested that this prediction could be tested by feeding animals with analogues of amino acids or RNA bases. Analogues are substances which are sufficiently similar to normal amino acids or RNA bases to be incorporated into newly synthesized protein or RNA molecules, but are different enough to impair the function of some of the molecules which contain them. Since they cause defects in function, incorporation of low levels of these analogues should, if Orgel's hypothesis is correct, initiate an error catastrophe which results in premature senescence.

It was found that feeding *Drosophila* larvae with amino-acid analogues for short periods did indeed shorten the life-span of the imagoes. However, later work showed that, contrary to prediction, feeding adult flies with amino-acid analogues had no effect on their life-span, even though there was evidence that the analogues had been incorporated into proteins. It was suggested, therefore, that larval feeding may have been effective in shortening adult life-span, not because an error catastrophe was initiated, but rather because some of the long-lived proteins which are formed in the pre-adult stages are not replaced in adult flies contained analogue and were therefore less efficient.

The results from experiments in which human fibroblast cultures have been treated with analogues are also rather ambiguous. Cultures treated with the RNA base analogue 5-fluoruracil were found to have a shorter life-span than normal, and the changes in proteins paralleled those found in naturally ageing cultures. However, Ryan *et al.* (1974) found that continuous exposure to non-toxic concentrations of amino-acid analogues did not affect culture life-span, even though the analogues were incorporated into proteins. Short exposures to toxic concentrations, i.e. concentrations which inhibited growth, also had no effect on the total doubling potential of these cells. Only prolonged treatment with toxic doses affected doubling potential significantly. It is difficult to see how these results can be reconciled with the error catastrophe hypothesis.

Perhaps the best evidence in favour of the error catastrophe hypothesis has come from work with fungi which show clonal senescence. As well as showing that amino-acid analogues shorten the life-span of *Podospora* and increase the amount of defective enzyme produced, Holliday and his colleagues have studied some mutant strains which show senescence. In particular, the results obtained with the *leu-5* mutant of *Neurospora* seem to provide good evidence for the error catastrophe hypothesis. This mutant produces an abnormal leucyl-tRNA synthetase molecule which charges leucyl-tRNA with other amino acids. As a result, many proteins are mistranslated because the tRNA molecules insert wrong amino acids into growing polypeptide chains. The *leu-5* strain does not show senescence at 20–25°C, but when it is transferred to 37° growth continues normally for only 3–4 days and then suddenly stops. Lewis and Holliday (1970) thought that this might be due to the faulty tRNA synthetase molecules initiating an error catastrophe. They tested this idea by measuring the amount of defective protein present at different times during the life-span at 35°C. Some of their results are given in figure 8.2 which shows the changing proportion of active glutamic dehydrogenase relative to the amount of immunologically detectable enzyme. On being transferred to 35° there is a rapid loss of enzyme activity during the first 10 hours. The proportion of inactive enzyme

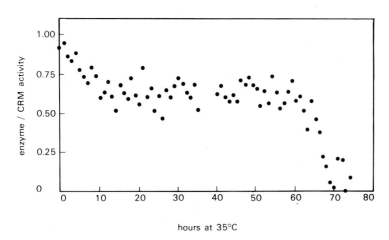

hours at 35°C

Figure 8.2   Age-related changes in the amount of inactive glutamic dehydrogenase produced by the *leu-5* strain of *Neurospora crassa* grown at 35°C (redrawn from Lewis and Holliday, 1970)

remains constant for the next 50 hours, but there is then a further dramatic decrease in enzyme activity. This suggests that after the initial increase in the amount of faulty protein produced following transfer to 35°C there is a constant level of mistranslation. However, by age 60 h the faulty translation has spread to other enzymes in the translation machinery, so that more and more faulty glutamic dehydrogenase molecules are produced. Heat-lability measurements also showed that the enzyme produced in old cultures at 35°C was different from that produced in young cultures. Moreover, the *leu-5* genotype was found to have mutator activity at 35°C. Since mistranslation would be expected to affect the enzymes involved in replicating the DNA during nuclear division (and thus make DNA replication inaccurate), the mutator activity of *leu-5* is further evidence supporting the idea that this gene may cause senescence by inducing extensive errors in protein synthesis.

8.3   Generalized error theories

The experiments described in the last section show that many of the predictions of Orgel's error catastrophe hypothesis have been found to be correct. Although the evidence is not totally consistent, it has been found that the cytoplasm is important in senescence, and that in situations where there is an increase in protein error frequency the life-span may be shorter. There are also many data showing that the quality of proteins in old animals or cell cultures is different from that in young animals or cultures. Nevertheless, as Orgel (1973) and other people have pointed out, the existence of these altered proteins in senescent cells and tissues is not in itself evidence that protein synthesis is inaccurate. Faulty proteins could be a consequence rather than a cause of senescence. For example, old cells may be less efficient at getting rid of defective proteins than young cells. Alternatively, proteins in old cells may be more liable to suffer post-synthetic modification than those in young cells, because protein turnover is lower and there is therefore more time for alterations to occur. The higher proportion of defective protein detected in old cultures or tissues could also be caused by the presence of a higher proportion of dead or dying cells. Dead or dying cells might contain more partially degraded proteins as a result of lysosomal enzyme activity. Thus, although it is difficult to decide which of the possible causes of defective proteins is in fact the reason for their existence in old cells, it is clear that they need not be the result of an error catastrophe.

Evidence against the theory that error catastrophes are the cause of cell culture senescence has come from work in which viruses have been used to test the ability of cells to replicate, translate, and transcribe genetic information. Virus multiplication depends on the host cells' synthesizing machinery. If ageing cells synthesize abnormal proteins, then viral replication and assembly should be affected because the viral genetic information will be inadequately replicated and translated. Holland and his colleagues (1973) found that senescent cells were just as capable as young cells of supporting virus replication. Furthermore, the thermal stability of viruses grown in early and late-passage fibroblasts was the same, indicating that there was no change in the proportion of abnormal virus-specified structural proteins produced by the senescent cells. Viruses grown in young and old cells also had similar mutation rates. This makes it unlikely that defective replicase molecules are present in old cells. These experiments therefore suggest that generalized errors in protein synthesis are not the cause of cell culture senescence.

As a result of the anomalies and ambiguities in the tests of the protein synthesis error theory, many people, including Orgel himself, are tending to favour a rather more generalized type of error theory of ageing (Medvedev 1967, Orgel 1973). Errors in protein synthesis may be only one of a whole spectrum of random molecular mistakes which could generate further errors. Mutations in nuclear or mitochondrial DNA, free-radical-induced membrane damage, cross-linkages between or within molecules such as nucleoproteins, and so on, could be as effective in generating a catastrophic accumulation of errors and damage as mistakes in protein synthesis alone. For example, in the same way that an error in a tRNA molecule might have effects on many different proteins and even on DNA, it is not difficult to see how damage to a lysosome membrane could, if it resulted in the release of lysosomal enzymes which damaged proteins, DNA and more membranes, initiate a catastrophic sequence of events leading to tissue damage or cell death. Similarly, changes in extracellular molecules could, if they reduced the efficiency of transport to and from cells, enhance the likelihood of damage within cells. This intracellular damage could, in turn, affect the formation of the extracellular material. In other words, many types of molecular damage are potentially capable of causing a chain reaction leading to further damage.

Hahn (1970) has proposed another molecular mechanism which might lead to senescence. It is known that there is an increase in the stability of DNA-histone binding in old cells. This may be due to increased cross-linking between the molecules (chapter 6). Since histones are believed to be involved in the regulation of gene activity, Hahn suggested that this increased binding might prevent the DNA from being transcribed into mRNA. The amount of genetic information available to the cell will therefore be reduced, and this will inevitably affect cellular efficiency. Again, what at first seem to be rather small molecular changes could in fact have profound consequences if the regulation mechanisms of the cell are affected.

8.4   Elimination of error-containing cells

If errors occur spontaneously and can lead to further errors, why is it that *all* cell lineages do not die out? How is it that HeLa cell cultures can continue to multiply indefinitely? More importantly, how do germ cells escape from the apparent inevitability of senescence?

It seems likely that many cells which contain defects are selected against both *in vivo* and *in vitro* because they grow more slowly and divide less frequently than non-defective cells. A cell line dies out only if, on the average, each cell produces less than one viable descendent. Considerable selection between defective and non-defective cells can therefore occur in cultures or *in vivo*. However, it is probably possible for cells to contain defective molecules which do not affect their ability to divide and compete with normal cells. In simple symmetrical division during logarithmic growth (figure 7.6B) cells containing such faulty molecules, or the breakdown products of faulty structures, will pass them to both of their daughter cells. Gradually, therefore, a whole clone of cells should come to contain more and more defective molecules and waste products, and die out.

Sheldrake (1974) has suggested that if instead of dividing symmetrically cells divide asymmetrically, it might allow cell lineages to continue without accumulating defective structures or waste products. If asymmetrical division occurs so that one of the daughter cells receives the faulty structures and waste products and is therefore committed to ultimate death, the other daughter cell will be rejuvenated. In situations where a stem cell divides to give a further stem cell and a cell which differentiates (the tangential model shown in figure 7.6A), it may be the latter which receives the accumulated "garbage" so that the stem cell is left relatively free of defects. One of the interesting points which Sheldrake makes is that in sexual reproduction in both plants and animals, where nearly all the cytoplasm of the zygote is provided by the egg, only one of the four products of meiosis gives rise to an egg. The three sister cells die. Sheldrake suggests that this may be a way of getting rid of deleterious products and thus freeing the germ line from cytoplasmic garbage.

Holliday (1975) has suggested another way in which the immortality of the germ line might be ensured in spite of the inevitability of the accumulation of molecular mistakes. He postulated that a special quality-control system might operate in germ cells. These cells could synthesize a protein which has no function in its normal form but would become a "suicide protein" which kills the cell if it contains incorrect amino acids. Such a suicide protein could be one which irreversibly turned off an important gene. This type of system would allow discrimination between cells containing errors in the protein synthesis apparatus and those which did not, and hence would ensure that defective gametes were selected against.

Holliday and his colleagues have also made some interesting calculations about the behaviour of cells in culture which show how (i) culture size, (ii) the probability that a critical error committing a clone to mortality will occur, and (iii) the number of cell divisions between initiation of the critical event and the ultimate death of the clone, all affect the likelihood of a culture continuing. One of the rather paradoxical conclusions that came from these calculations is that cultures of transformed cells may be immortal because errors can build up more rapidly in these cells than in normal diploid cells. The reason for this is that if the number of divisions between the initiation of the critical event which irreversibly commits a cell's descendents to death and the actual death of the clone is high, the culture will come to consist of more and more committed cells. Selection between committed and uncommitted cells cannot occur until death or a reduction in proliferation rate takes place. By the time that this reduction in division rate occurs, it may be too late for the culture to survive, because all the uncommitted cells will have been diluted out by the subculturing technique. On the other hand, if after the initiating event the build-up of errors is so rapid that the cells die shortly afterwards, selection between committed and uncommitted cells will occur. The uncommitted cells will continue to grow and divide and will predominate in the culture. Thus, in cultures of limited size, for the same rate of initiation of critical errors, rapid build-up of further errors will be associated with immortality, whereas slow build-up of errors will be associated with a limited culture life-span. Transformed cells might build up errors more rapidly if, for example, they are less efficient at repairing or degrading defective molecules. Thus "inferior" cells could have the longest clonal life-span.

8.5 Repair and elimination of error-containing molecules

Although in renewing or expanding tissues selection between cells may enable those with defects to be eliminated and replaced by new cells, cell replacement obviously cannot occur in non-renewing tissues. For this reason alone it would be expected that, since it seems likely that metabolic errors are inevitable, selection would favour mechanisms which repair damaged molecules or structures, or break them down into metabolically inactive forms.

There is a growing body of evidence suggesting that cells are indeed capable of eliminating or repairing damaged molecules. We have already considered the accumulation of lipofuscin in cells of old animals. This pigment is possibly the end-product left after the breakdown of cell organelles containing membranes which have suffered peroxidation damage. Although the accumulation of this pigment may ultimately affect cellular function, it seems likely that it is less detrimental than damaged mitochondria or endoplasmic reticulum would be.

There is evidence that *Escherichia coli* has a mechanism for the selective degradation of abnormal proteins. In this bacterium incomplete polypeptide chains, proteins which contain translation errors induced by mutations affecting ribosomes or tRNA specificity, and proteins containing amino-acid analogues, are all degraded more rapidly than normal cell proteins. It is becoming clear that the cells of eukaryotes also have a comparable system for scavenging faulty proteins (Goldberg and Dice, 1974).

It has been known for a long time that the cells of eukaryotes are able to repair damaged DNA. Largely as a result of studies of the repair of damage produced by exposure to ionizing and ultraviolet radiation, several different mechanisms for DNA repair have been identified. The details of these mechanisms are not important for our present discussion, but it is important to realize that different enzyme systems are involved in the various types of repair. Thus a cell may be capable of repairing ultraviolet-induced damage, but not damage produced by X-radiation, and *vice versa*.

Recently a great deal of interest has been shown in the possibility that defective or deficient repair of DNA damage may be one of the causes of ageing. It has been found that old tissues do show evidence of an accumulation of DNA damage. For example, Price *et al.* (1971) found that nuclear DNA in sections from a number of different tissues from old mice had a higher template activity for calf thymus DNA polymerase than that in young tissues. DNA polymerase catalyses the synthesis of a complementary strand to single-stranded regions of DNA. Therefore, if tissues are incubated with DNA polymerase and radioactivity-labelled DNA precursors, the amount of radioactive label incorporated into the nuclei is a measure of the amount of single-stranded DNA present. Table 8.2 shows that the amount of label incorporated was greater for nuclei in old tissues than it was for

Table 8.2 DNA polymerase catalysed incorporation of radioactive DNA precursors into cells of old and young mice (data of Price *et al*, 1971).

Cell type	Mean grain count per nucleus			
	Young		Old	
	Undenatured	*Acid denatured*	*Undenatured*	*Acid denatured*
Neurones and astrocytes	8.92	30	22.13	very high
Liver Kupffer cells	2	4.5	6.28	13.9
Cardiac muscle	0.67	1.58	3.5	8.63

those in young tissues. This indicates that senescent-cell DNA contains more single-strand breaks than young-cell DNA.

Confirmation of this observation has come from work with beagles. By using a completely different technique, Wheeler and Lett (1974) found that the molecular size of the DNA extracted from tissues of old dogs was smaller than that from young dogs. This too suggests that old DNA has more breaks than young DNA. However, when additional breaks were induced by radiation, it was found that old and young dogs were equally capable of restoring these breaks. Therefore, although there is evidence that DNA in old animals contains more strand breaks than that in young animals, this may not be because old cells are less capable of repairing DNA damage. It might be that the DNA in old cells suffers more damage due to increased lysosomal enzyme activity or free radical attack. Whatever the cause of the increase in strand breaks, these breaks are probably detrimental to cell function, since they may affect the ability of RNA polymerase to transcribe some messages from DNA.

One case where an association between ageing and defective DNA repair has been found is in fibroblast cells from people suffering from Hutchinson-Gilford progeria (Epstein *et al.*, 1973). These cells have been shown to be defective in their ability to repair X-ray-induced DNA damage, and the cultures also have very short life-spans. However, it may be incorrect to deduce from this that deficient DNA repair is the cause of the reduced life-span of the patients or of their cells. Xeroderma pigmentosum is another genetic disease which is associated with defective DNA repair. Patients usually die from multiple skin cancers, since their skin is abnormally sensitive to sunlight. It has been shown that their cells cannot repair the DNA damage induced by ultraviolet radiation. Nevertheless, sufferers from this disease do not show signs of progeria, and the life-span of cultures of their fibroblasts is not abnormally short. Therefore deficient DNA repair is certainly not always associated with premature senescence.

In normal fibroblast cultures, the ability to repair DNA damage does not decline until relatively late in culture life-span. Since it occurs so late in the life-span, this decline is probably a consequence of some of the other changes which we have discussed in this chapter, rather than the cause of the culture death.

At present, therefore, although we know that DNA damage increases with age, there is little reason for believing that there is an age-related deterioration in repair capacity. It must be remembered, however, that although old cells may still be able to repair their DNA, the quality of the repair may not be the same as in young cells.

8.6 The molecular basis for species differences in longevity

All of the theories of ageing which we have considered so far in this chapter suggest that the deterioration associated with old age is due to the accumulation of random molecular damage. It is known that some types of damage can certainly be repaired, but we know little about the repair or elimination of damage in molecules other than DNA.

Although these theories which attribute ageing to random damage and error accumulation provide an explanation for the age-related decline in functional abilities of cells and tissues, and hence of the whole animal, additional assumptions have to be made if they are also to explain the fact that different species have different characteristic life-spans. It is necessary to postulate either (i) that the molecules in the cells and tissues of some species are less likely to suffer from damage than those of other species, or (ii) that species differ in their abilities to repair damage, or (iii) that some species are more able to tolerate damage than others. It seems likely that all three ideas are to some extent correct.

It is not difficult to think of reasons why molecules in some species may be more susceptible to damage than those in others. Even small genetic differences may affect the structure of molecules in ways which make them more or less liable to free-radical attack and cross-linkage damage. The genetic differences which determine metabolic rate are also likely to cause differences in damage rate. Dietary differences between species may influence the rate at which damage accumulates if some diets contain more free-radical inhibitors than others. Clearly, many factors will influence the rate at which damage accumulates in different species.

Recently it has been shown that species also differ in their ability to repair at least one type of damage. Hart and Setlow (1974) compared the capacity of fibroblasts from seven mammalian species to repair DNA damage induced by ultraviolet radiation. The fibroblasts were all obtained from the superficial dermis of animals which had completed about a twentieth of their life-span. After establishing the cultures, the cells were irradiated and grown in a medium containing radioactive thymidine and hydroxyurea. Hydroxyurea almost completely inhibits normal DNA replication but permits DNA repair. Therefore the amount of radioactive label incorporated into each nucleus when hydroxyurea is present is a measurement of the amount of repair that is occurring. Hart and Setlow found that in all species the amount of repair detected depended on the U-V radiation dose and on the time that the cells were incubated with the radioactive label, but at all doses it increased rapidly immediately after irradiation and had reached a final maximum value after 12 h incubation. Their most important observation was that both the initial rate of repair and the final level reached are species-dependent (figure 8.3). At all doses used, there was an excellent correlation between species life-span and the amount of radioactive label incorporated into the fibroblast nuclei. Since there is evidence that the amount of DNA per cell is similar in all the mammals, and that the amount of damage caused by a given dose of ultraviolet radiation is also similar, Hart and Setlow's data suggest that the rate and extent of repair of ultraviolet-induced DNA damage is strongly species-dependent and is related to life-span.

Species differences in the ability of animals to tolerate molecular damage rather than to repair it could also be a reason for their different life-spans. Medvedev (1972) has discussed this possibility in some detail, particularly with reference to DNA damage and gene repetition. It is known that many of the genes in normal diploid animals are present in multiple copies. For example, the genes which code for rRNAs and tRNAs are repeated many times in most species. Medvedev cites data which show that the number of repetitions of genes for the major rRNA is 5–10 in bacteria, 100–130 in *Drosophila* species, and 250–600 in vertebrates. Some mRNAs are also known to be present in repeated copies. In fact, in higher animals the amount of repetition of nucleotide sequences in nuclear DNA is very high. Medvedev believes that the amount of repetition of genetic information might be an important determinant of longevity because, if a gene is repeated many times, damage in some copies of it will be less important than damage in genes which are not repeated. According to Medvedev,

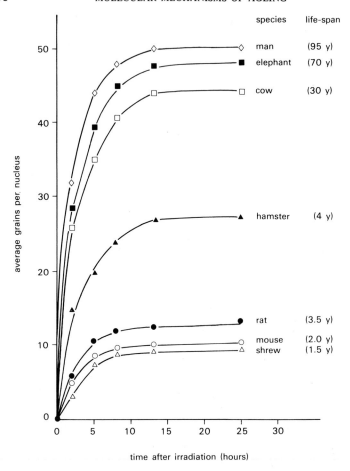

Figure 8.3 The repair of DNA damage following irradiation of fibroblasts from seven different species with ultraviolet light (redrawn from Hart and Setlow, 1974).

age-related deterioration is likely to be due primarily to damage in non-repeated DNA sequences. Therefore, the greater the proportion of the genome present in repeated sequences, the greater the chances of survival. Repetition of genes may be a protective device against the accumulation of random errors in DNA.

Medvedev suggests that this idea that longevity is a function of the amount of repetition of information can be extended to other molecules. For example, protein molecules may be short-lived or long-lived. Short-lived proteins can be thought of as molecules which are repeated in time. Since they are short-lived and are constantly replaced, damage to them will be less important than damage to long-lived molecules which are not replaced. Similarly the argument can be extended to cells which are replaced, i.e. are repeated in time, and those which are not. Damage in cells in renewing tissues is less likely to cause the deterioration of the animal than is damage in non-replaceable fixed post-mitotic cells.

Medvedev's hypothesis that gene repetition may enable cells to tolerate some DNA damage is difficult to test experimentally. However, it is interesting to note that Johnson et al. (1972) have found that there is a reduction in one type of repeated DNA sequence in some cell types in old beagles. They found that the amount of DNA coding for rRNA in nuclei of the brain, heart and skeletal muscle decreased with age, whereas that in the cells of mitotic tissue did not. They believe that the reduction in the amount of DNA coding for rRNA may be due to misrepair of DNA damage, and that it could be the reason for the loss of cells in non-renewing tissues. Whatever the cause of this loss of DNA, the data do suggest that cells can tolerate a considerable reduction in the number of copies of a repeated gene. It is therefore consistent with Medvedev's hypothesis that repeated genes may protect cells against molecular damage.

Cutler (1974) has looked for correlations between the amount of reiterated DNA and the life-span of mammalian species. He found no clear correlation between the percentage of reiterated DNA and longevity, or between the amount of ribosomal gene redundancy and the rate of ageing. However, when he looked at the genes involved in transcribing mRNA in the brain of mice, cows and humans, he found that the average redundancy was greater in humans than in cows, and greater in cows than in mice. This is what would be expected if repeated mRNA genes allow cells to tolerate DNA damage.

8.7   Development, differentiation, and programmed senescence

Provided that enough assumptions are made about the rate of accumulation of damage and the ability of cells to repair or tolerate damaged molecules, error and damage theories of ageing can explain, or at least are compatible with, many of the facts of animal senescence. Nevertheless, many people find it difficult to believe that this type of theory is sufficient to account for all types of ageing change and senescence. For example, it is difficult to see how random changes can account for the senescence and longevity differences shown by different cell types within the body. Why should epidermal cells, gut mucosal cells and erythrocytes have different characteristic life-spans? It seems probable that the longevity and senescence of these cells is determined by the genetic programme in a rather more direct way than is assumed in random damage theories of ageing. If so, why should not all cell life-spans be genetically programmed, and why should not these programmes determine the life-span of the animal?

Theories which relate ageing to the genetic programme are very varied and often rather vague. The most plausible are those which suggest that senescence`is a consequence of differentiation and development, i.e. that senescence is the "price paid" for differentiation.

One of the most detailed of the genetic theories of senescence is that which has been put forward by Strehler (1967). Unlike so many of the others, it is testable. Basically, it suggests that as a result of differentiation cells lose the ability to translate genetic information. Most people now see development and differentiation as a programmed sequential turning on and off of different sets of genes, but how this is brought about is not known. Strehler's *codon-restriction* hypothesis suggests one possible way in which the amount and type of proteins synthesized at different times, or by different cells, might be controlled by the genetic programme. It is a rather complicated hypothesis, but it is based on the fact that the genetic code is degenerate. That is to say, each of the 20 amino acids which make up proteins can be specified by more than one triplet of DNA bases. For example, the mRNA transcribed from DNA contains the four nucleosides uridine (U), adenosine (A), cytidine (C) and guanosine (G); the triplets GUU, GUC, GUA and GUG all code for the amino-acid valine. Since several different triplets (codons) are used for each amino acid, it was postulated, and later proved, that several types of tRNA exist for each amino acid, and probably that several types of tRNA synthetase are involved in charging the different tRNA molecules with the amino acid.

The fact that the genetic code is degenerate led Strehler to propose that the proteins synthesized by a cell might be determined by the types of tRNA or, more probably, by the types of tRNA synthetase present. A cell which has no tRNA synthetase or tRNA for an amino acid coded by a particular triplet would be unable to translate any of the messages which use that codon; it could translate messages for other proteins containing the same amino acid provided a different codon was used. Thus a cell might be able to produce the proteins containing valine coded by GUU, but not those containing valine specified by the GUG codon.

If the set of tRNAs and tRNA synthetases that a cell contains determines the messages that it can translate, many of the sequential changes seen during differentiation can be explained. The tRNA synthetases are themselves proteins, and messages for them have to be translated. At any point in time, the genes that a cell is capable of translating will depend on the tRNA synthetases which have been synthesized previously, and the tRNA synthetase genes that are currently being translated will in turn determine the genes which can be translated in the future. Thus during differentiation there will be sequential changes in the spectrum of tRNA synthetases produced, and consequently changes in the codons translated and in the proteins that the cell synthesizes. In practise the system that Strehler envisages may also involve tRNA synthetase repressors and more complex interactions, but the essential feature of the model is that through a feed-back system there will be a serial modification of the codon sets which the cell can translate.

Strehler believes that if differentiation is programmed in this way it will lead to senescence because a differentiated cell will have lost the ability to translate certain messages which it could have translated at an earlier stage of development. It will no longer have the appropriate tRNAs or tRNA synthetases to translate these messages. If some of the proteins which were produced at an earlier stage of differentiation deteriorate, then the cell will be unable to produce replacements for them, even though it still contains all the necessary genetic information for their production, because the decoding machinery which is in operation is not able to translate the messages. Thus, the mechanism which brings about differentiation will also result in senescence because it irreversibly closes down parts of the translation machinery.

Since Strehler developed his codon-restriction hypothesis, evidence has been obtained which shows that some of its predictions are correct (see Andron and Strehler 1973). As would be expected, the complement of tRNAs and tRNA synthetases is not the same in all tissues, e.g. calf spleen contains only one of the two histidine tRNAs that are present in the liver. It is also known that alterations in the translation machinery occur during development. So far there is no evidence that there are differences between the types of tRNA and tRNA synthetases present in the tissues of old and young animals, but in plant cotyledons it has been shown that ageing is accompanied by changes in the types of tRNA synthetases present. Thus, although much more experimental testing is required, Strehler's hypothesis does seem to provide a useful working model for differentiation and cell senescence.

Acceptance or rejection of the idea that senescence is a consequence of differentiation and development does not, of course, depend on the acceptance or rejection of the particular model that Strehler has proposed.

Moreover, even if the idea that senescence is the result of the genetic programme that brings about differentiation is accepted, it does not mean that error and damage (stochastic) theories of ageing have to be rejected. After all, Strehler's model suggests that the ultimate failure and death of a cell will be due to damage to irreplaceable molecules. The difference between stochastic and programmed theories of ageing is often a difference of approach and emphasis more than anything else. Although some people strongly support programmed ageing theories and others champion stochastic theories, it may be wiser to think of the two types of theory as complementing each other rather than as alternatives.

CHAPTER NINE

CONCLUSIONS

THERE IS NO GENERAL AGREEMENT ABOUT THE FUNDAMENTAL CAUSE OR CAUSES of ageing. Although there are many different ideas about how and why it may happen, no single theory is capable of explaining all the known facts. However, if the arguments about the evolution of senescence that we considered in chapter 3 are correct, then there is no real reason why we should expect a single cause of all ageing phenomena. Ageing may be the result of the accumulation of damage and defects of diverse origins; *all* of the many causes of ageing which have been suggested may contribute to the deterioration found in old age. The structural and functional interrelations of the various components of cells, tissues and organs may make the end results of different types of damage very similar.

In this final chapter an attempt will be made to summarize some of the ideas discussed earlier by assuming that senescence is caused by accumulated damage, and that the rate at which damage accumulates can be modified by both genetic and environmental factors.

9.1 The events leading to senescence

Figure 9.1 shows the chain of events which might result from accidental damage in cellular macromolecules. It is assumed that:

1a. At the molecular level, accidents are inevitable (e.g. cross-linkages will occur within and between molecules; DNA bases will be damaged; errors will be made in transcription and translation of genetic information).
   b. The interrelations between molecules are such that some types of damaged molecules are likely to induce defects in other molecules (e.g. errors in DNA polymerases may cause defective DNA replication leading to base changes in DNA; defective tRNA molecules will produce defective proteins).
2a. As a result of molecular defects, subcellular functions will become inefficient (e.g. damaged membrane lipids will affect mitochondrial function; cross-linkages in nucleoproteins may prevent DNA transcription; enzyme defects will affect general cell metabolism).
   b. Accumulated defects in extracellular macromolecules will change the cellular environ-

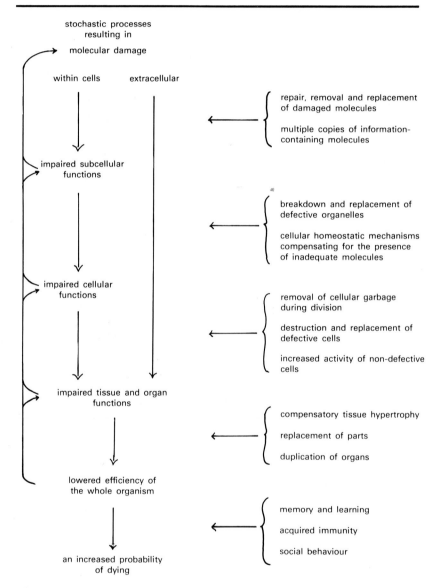

Figure 9.1 The events leading to senescence and death.

ment and tissue structure (e.g. cross-linkages in elastin and collagen may affect tissue flexibility; changes in the extracellular matrix may lead to diffusion barriers).

3a. Decreased efficiency of subcellular functions will lead to a reduction in cell efficiency (e.g. inability to transcribe mRNA might prevent secretory cells from producing their products; mitochondrial defects are likely to affect all energy-requiring processes; nuclear changes may affect the ability of lymphocytes to proliferate in response to antigenic stimulation).

b. In some cases the decreased efficiency of subcellular functions will lead to cell death because the cell will no longer be able to maintain itself.

4. As a result of the decline in cell efficiency, cell death, and changes in the extracellular environment, the functional capacities of tissues, organs and organ systems will deteriorate (e.g. changes in nerve cells will affect brain function; changes in lymphocytes will make the immune system less efficient).

5. Deterioration in tissues and organs leads to deterioration of the whole organism (e.g. declining efficiency of the immune system will make animals less resistant to infectious diseases; deterioration of the neuromuscular system will reduce an animal's ability to get sufficient food and to escape predators).

6. Deterioration of the organism results in an increased probability of dying.

Although we have presented the sequence of events involved in ageing as a linear series, each succeeding step in the chain may have positive feedback effects on earlier stages. Thus if an animal cannot get sufficient food because of deterioration of the neuromuscular system, other types of cell may be starved of nutrients and will deteriorate. Similarly, defects in the immunological system may result in damage in other tissues as a result of infection. The system should be thought of as a network of reactions rather than as a simple chain of events.

Since molecular damage produced by stochastic processes is inevitable, a gradual accumulation of defects which ultimately lead to death must also be inevitable unless animals possess mechanisms which repair or counteract the adverse effects of damage. The right-hand side of figure 9.1 shows some of the ways in which the deleterious effects may be reduced or prevented from giving rise to more damage. Obviously, not all of these countermeasures are present in all animals. For example, there is no cell division in many adult insects so replacement of defective cells is impossible; social behaviour which gives protection and support to weak animals is probably limited to higher mammals. Furthermore, even within an animal, a particular protective device may not be found in all cells, tissues and organs. Thus mammals have two kidneys and complete deterioration of one can be tolerated, but there is no duplication of the heart; extensive cell replacement can occur in the liver, but not in the brain.

9.2 The influence of the environment

We have assumed that the initiating events in the sequence shown in the figure are all of spontaneous internal origin, but we know that ageing and longevity are also influenced by environmental factors. The environment will affect the system at all levels. It will affect the probability of dying because, in an environment in which there is plenty of food, few predators, and little competition, an old "inefficient" animal may survive, whereas in a harsher environment it could not.

Environmental factors will also have effects at the tissue and organ level. For example, some diets may lead to more rapid wear or decay of mammalian teeth, and this might lead to malnutrition. In insects, high temperatures increase the level of activity. Active insects are likely to suffer more cuticular damage, and this damage will affect cuticle permeability. If the environment is also dry, this could lead to water loss. Water loss would affect the osmotic and ionic composition of the body fluids and hence affect cell function adversely.

At the molecular level, the environment will affect the type and frequency of molecular accidents. High temperatures may increase the level of metabolic errors in poikilotherms because they increase metabolic rate; ionizing radiation will increase the damage in some types of molecule; a diet deficient in antioxidants may increase the damage caused by free radicals. Although high temperatures, ionizing radiation, and diets deficient in natural antioxidants may all increase the level of molecular damage and also shorten the life-span, this should not lead us to expect that all of the normal ageing changes will be accelerated to the same extent by all three factors. The changes seen will probably depend on the type of molecular damage that is enhanced by the environmental agent. For example, if one environment leads to an increased level of DNA damage and another environment causes an increased amount of damage to lipid membranes, the resulting effects on the ageing processes might be different. For the sake of argument, assume that DNA damage is more deleterious in cells which are capable of division than in those which are not, because it impairs the ability of cells to divide, and that membrane damage is more important in post-mitotic cells because they cannot dilute the breakdown products of damage by cell division. It follows from these assumptions that the animals which are subjected to an environment which increases DNA damage will show the greatest deterioration in their renewing tissues, whereas animals kept in an environment which increases membrane damage will manifest higher rates of functional decline in non-renewing tissues. The positive feedback in the system will mean that there will be a considerable overlap in the spectrum of changes seen in each environment, but not all "natural" ageing changes will be accelerated to the same extent. Both environments nevertheless affect the "natural" ageing processes.

The life-span of mammals can be prolonged by restricting the intake of calories. How can the life-prolonging effect of calorie restriction be interpreted in terms of the scheme shown in figure 9.1? Cutler (1972) has suggested that restricted diets lower specific metabolic rate and slightly lower the temperature of the extremities. This lower metabolic rate will, he suggested, decrease the rate of production of damage, and thus relatively more time will be available for the repair of the damage that is produced.

A similar argument can be used to explain the increase in imaginal longevity produced by lowering the rate of development in *Drosophila*. If development is slow, repair and replacement mechanisms will have more time in which to operate, and consequently the imago that develops contains fewer faults.

9.3 The influence of the genotype

The genotype of an individual has important influences on the scheme of events shown in figure 9.1. It affects both the probability that particular types of damage will occur, and also the extent of compensation, repair, or replacement.

Species differences in longevity and the rate of ageing must in some way be related to the genetic differences between species and to the evolutionary processes which led to these differences. According to the arguments presented in chapter 3, genes which are selected for the favourable effects that they have early in life may also have detrimental effects in later life. There is a lack of evolutionary pressure to prevent or ameliorate any deleterious changes which occur late in life, since few animals in natural environments survive to an old age. It is obvious that if these arguments are correct, ageing and development are intimately linked, and the nature of senescence may be determined primarily by the way in which development and reproduction have evolved. In the sense that all living systems depend ultimately on the genetic programme, senescence can be said to be programmed. However, it is probably better to regard senescence as the result of a running out of a life-maintaining programme rather than as the result of a positive programme for death.

At the cellular level, however, it is probable that death of some cell types is programmed and has been selected during evolution. Cell death plays an important part in development in many species, and many cell types in adult mammals have short determinate life-spans. It is not difficult to imagine how programmed cell death may have evolved. Consider a situation where, as a result of mutation, a particular type of long-lived cell becomes more efficient at a specialized function. Assume that this mutation is selected because the improved cell function makes the animal more vigorous, and it produces more offspring than an individual which lacks the mutation. Now assume that one of the side-effects of the change in activity of the cell type is that the cells with the mutation accumulate more metabolic errors and damage, and that their increased rate of deterioration reduces the life-span of the animal. Natural selection will then favour mechanisms which reduce the life-span limiting effects of this cell type. Selection for improved repair mechanisms might take place. Alternatively, there might be selection of animals which retain a large reserve of partially differentiated stem cells which can replace the defective cells. If this reserve capacity is available, there may be a selective advantage in any change which leads to rapid cell death before damage accumulates sufficiently to impair a cell's efficiency. For example, selection might favour a system whereby differentiation of the cell type is accompanied by a permanent repression of genes which code for some of the enzymes essential for cell maintenance. The cell life-span would then be limited by the life-span of the enzyme molecules and the mRNA which codes for them. The point is that, providing cell replacement can occur, programmed cell death could be an evolutionary advantage because it would lead to a rapid well-defined death phase without the prolonged deterioration in the cells' specialized functions that would result from the steady accumulation of damage from stochastic processes.

While it is fairly easy to see how selection could lead to programmed death of cells which can be replaced, it is difficult to see the selective advantage of systems which would limit the life-span of cells in non-renewing tissues. Since there is no opportunity to replace these cells, selection should favour mechanisms which prevent, repair, remove, or mitigate the effects of the damage which occurs in them.

As far as whole organisms are concerned, it is possible that positive selection for a limited life-span could occur through group selection but, as we have said, it seems more likely that the life-span characteristic of each species is to a large extent an indirect consequence of the evolution of the mechanisms which bring about development and reproductive maturity. Some evolutionary changes which improve vigour in youth may also lead to an increase in potential longevity. Thus selection for improved homeostatic mechanisms should tend to increase maximum longevity, because it improves survival chances at *all* ages. Selection for increased body size may result in a lower metabolic rate and hence increase longevity. However, selection for increased body size is more likely to occur because it improves the chances of reaching maturity and reproducing than because it increases the maximum length of life. It must be remembered that it is unlikely that many animals in natural conditions ever achieve their maximum longevity potential.

Some evolutionary changes that improve vigour in youth may reduce life-span. Insects which do not feed as adults do not "waste time" looking for food; all of their energies go into finding a mate and reproducing. Consequently, they must have short adult life-spans because they run out of materials for self-maintenance and repair. Thus the genetic changes which improve vigour in youth may have side effects which either increase or decrease longevity potential.

Even if the rate of ageing and maximum longevity of a species are determined primarily by the indirect effects of selection for vigour in youth, selection for increased longevity should still occur. Any small genetic changes which reduce the incidence of damage, improve the ability to repair damage, or provide protection against the effects of damage, should be favoured, provided that they do not have disadvantages of other kinds. Within a species, many of the inherited differences in the life-spans of individuals could be due to small variations in proteins, which result in differences in the probability that the molecules will suffer damage. Other genetically determined differences between individuals may influence the efficiency of repair or replacement of damaged molecules. Natural selection will utilize this type of variation to improve longevity potential. Nevertheless, the extent to which natural selection can improve survival by modifying repair and replacement mechanisms may be limited by the side-effects that these modifications would have. In chapter 7 we considered Dykhuizen's idea that selection may not favour immortality of cell lineages because an indefinite capacity for cell division would mean that cells which escape from their normal sites would be likely to form tumours capable of growing indefinitely. It has also been suggested that the accuracy of DNA replication and repair will not be allowed to become too good, because too efficient repair and replication enzymes would reduce the rate of production of new genetic variation within a species (see Burnet, 1974). If these ideas are correct, selection for the improvement of some of the possible repair and replacement mechanisms which could increase life-span will not take place.

As a result of natural selection, it would be expected that the times of failure in different component parts of an animal should become synchronized. There will be no great "evolutionary incentive" to improve the efficiency of repair, replacement or compensatory mechanisms in one part of the system unless it is accompanied by improvements in other parts. Thus, although delaying the deterioration of visual capacities may improve the

M

prospects of survival, selection for a reduction in the rate of decline in visual functions is unlikely to be very strong if the animals concerned die because their teeth wear out. Selection for delaying the decline in visual functions and improving the survival of teeth will tend to go together. Slight improvements in one system will enhance the selective advantages of improvements in another.

The same type of argument could also be applied to deterioration at the cellular and molecular level. The survival capacity of a nerve cell may be increased if mechanisms which reduce the likelihood of an error catastrophe improve, but selection for improvements in this system will not be strong if the cell accumulates DNA damage rapidly. Selection for more efficient repair of DNA (or additional copies of important genes) should accompany selection of mechanisms which reduce the probability of translation errors. Similarly, selection for improving the proliferative capacity of stem cells in the skin, gut, or bone marrow will not be strong if an animal's life-span is limited by the deterioration of non-renewing tissues.

If the arguments outlined above are correct, then we would expect to find that, for animals with a similar basic design, there are correlations between longevity and *many* of the different genetically determined factors which affect the rate of accumulation and repair of damage. The correlations may not be very close, because there may be more than one way of improving some particular part of the system. For example, *either* more efficient DNA repair *or* repeated genes may preserve essential genetic messages. Nevertheless, general correlations would be expected and have indeed been found. Longevity is correlated with the ability to repair U-V damage; long-lived mammals tend to accumulate chromosome aberrations more slowly (presumably because they have better repair mechanisms); there is a little evidence that long-lived species have more copies of some important genes; the doubling potential of fibroblasts seems to be associated with species longevity. If selection has acted in the way that we have suggested, further correlations should be found.

9.4 Can we modify human ageing and longevity?

Although some of the arguments that we have been considering in this chapter are rather speculative and may indeed be wrong, most gerontologists would probably accept the basic ideas that many different types of damage contribute to ageing changes, and that there are complex interactions between the changes which occur in the molecules, cells, tissues and organ systems during ageing. If the processes leading to senescence are so generalized and so complex, it might be thought that searching for the causes of ageing in the hope of finding a cure is a pointless task. It probably is true that we shall never discover an "elixir of life" which will prevent senescence, or even that we shall be able to extend maximum life span by many years. Perhaps we should not wish to do so, since the social and economic problems that this type of "advance" would create would be enormous. Most gerontologists in fact have the rather more modest and realistic hope that by studying the nature and causes of ageing processes they will discover ways of alleviating the more unpleasant symptoms of senescence and improving the chances of remaining vigorous in old age.

It is conceivable that we could retard ageing processes slightly by environmental manipulation. Our present knowledge suggests that this might be achieved by dietary control, or possibly by slightly lowering body temperature. Both these methods might reduce the rate of damage accumulation at the molecular level and thus increase longevity. The human survival curve would be shifted to the right.

It is far more likely, however, that in the foreseeable future the greatest impact of gerontology will be in the area of improving the methods of counteracting or compensating for ageing changes. This is something which has already been happening for many years and has led to the change in the survival curve from the diagonal type which describes the mortality statistics of C19 populations to the rectangular curve which is characteristic of populations in modern developed countries. This change in the shape of the survival curve has been brought about by two factors. Firstly, the hazards to which people have been exposed have been reduced. For example, improved public health measures have lowered the chances of suffering from cholera and typhoid fever. Unfortunately it is also true that some new hazards have been created in industrial societies, e.g. those due to environmental pollution. However, on balance, there has been an overall reduction in the factors which are likely to cause early death. The second reason for the change in the shape of the survival curve is that medical advances have enabled supplements or additions to be made to some of the counter-measures which are listed in the right-hand part of figure 9.1 We can now supply new artificial replacement parts such as false teeth or artificial limbs. Spectacles and hearing aids can compensate for the decreasing efficiency of eyes and ears. By surgery or radiation treatment we can destroy defective cells and tissues, and organ and tissue transplants are now possible. We can remedy failures in some cell and organ functions by, for example, blood transfusions or insulin injections. Antibiotics can be used to supplement the immune system.

Most of these measures are used only when deterioration has already shown itself as a decrease in functional efficiency. The challenge to gerontologists is to identify the more fundamental causes of the deterioration. If we can do this, then it may be possible to prevent or reduce the rate of decrease in functional efficiency in at least some systems. Even preventing damage accumulation and improving natural repair in a few systems will allow many more people to look forward to and enjoy a healthier old age.

BIBLIOGRAPHY

General References

Burnet, M. (1974) *Intrinsic Mutagenesis: a Genetic Approach to Ageing*, Medical and Technical Publishing, Lancaster.

Comfort, A. (1964) *Ageing: the Biology of Senescence*, Routledge and Kegan Paul, London.

Curtis, H. J. (1966) *Biological Mechanisms of Aging*, Ch. C. Thomas, Illinois.

Kohn, R. R. (1971) *Principles of Mammalian Aging*, Prentice-Hall, New Jersey.

Strehler, B. L. (1962) *Time, Cells and Aging*, Academic Press, New York and London.

Timiras, P. S. (1972) *Developmental Physiology and Aging*, Macmillan, New York.

Chapter 1

Comfort, A. (1960) in "Discussion Session I. Definition and universality of aging", in *The Biology of Aging* (ed. Strehler, B. L.) Am. Inst. Biol. Sci., Washington, 3–13.

Maynard Smith, J. (1962) "Review lectures on senescence. I. The causes of ageing", *Proc. R. Soc. Lond., Ser. B*, **157**, 115–127.

Medawar, P. B. (1946) "Old age and natural death", reprinted in *The Uniqueness of the Individual*, Methuen, London, 1957, 17–43.

Medawar, P. B. (1952) "An unsolved problem of biology", reprinted in *The Uniqueness of the Individual*, Methuen, London, 1957, 44–70.

Chapter 2

Baxter, R. C. and Blair, H. A. (1967) "Kinetics of aging as revealed by X-ray-dose – lethality relations in *Drosophila*", *Radiat. Res.*, **30**, 48–70.

Comfort, A. (1969) "Test-battery to measure ageing-rate in man", *Lancet*, **2**, 1411–1415.

Crosfill, M. L., Lindop, P. J. and Rotblat, J. (1959) "Variation of sensitivity to ionizing radiation with age", *Nature*, **183**, 1729–1730.

Flückiger, E. and Verzár, F. (1955) "Lack of adaptation to low oxygen pressure in aged animals", *J. Gerontol.*, **10**, 306-311.

Grahame, R. and Holt, P. J. L. (1969) "The influence of ageing on the *in vivo* elasticity of human skin", *Gerontologia*, **15**, 121–139.

Hollingsworth, J. W., Hashizume, A. and Jablon, S. (1965) "Correlations between tests of aging in Hiroshima subjects – an attempt to define 'physiologic age' ", *Yale J. Biol. Med.*, **38**, 11–26.

Keogh, E. V. and Walsh, R. J. (1965) "Rate of greying of human hair", *Nature*, **207**, 877–878.

Shock, N. W. (1974) "Physiological theories of aging", in *Theoretical Aspects of Aging* (ed. M. Rockstein) Academic Press, New York and London, 119–136.

Storer, J. B. (1965) "Mean homeostatic levels as a function of age and genotype", in *Aging and Levels of Biological Organization* (eds. A. M. Brues and G. A. Sacher) University of Chicago Press, Chicago and London, 192–205.

Chapter 3

Deevey, E. S. (1947) "Life tables for natural populations of animals", *Q. Rev. Biol.*, **22**, 283–314.

Hamilton, W. D. (1966) "The moulding of senescence by natural selection", *J. Theor. Biol.*, **12**, 12–45.

Medawar, P. B. (1955) "The definition and measurement of senescence", in *Ciba Foundation Colloquia on Ageing. I. General Aspects* (eds. Wolstenholme, G. E. W. and Cameron, M. P.) Churchill, London, 4–15.

Registrar General's Decennial Supplement, England and Wales, 1961, *Life Tables*, Her Majesty's Stationery Office, 1968.

Williams, G. C. (1957) "Pleiotropy, natural selection, and the evolution of senescence", *Evolution*, **11**, 398–411.

Wynne-Edwards, V. C. (1962) *Animal Dispersion in Relation to Social Behaviour*, Oliver and Boyd, Edinburgh and London.

Chapter 4

Abbott, M. H., Murphy, E. A., Bolling, D. R. and Abbey, H. (1974) "The familial component in longevity: a study of nonagenarians. II. Preliminary analysis of the completed study", *John Hopkins Med. J.*, **134**, 1–16.

Altman, P. A. and Dittmer, D. S. (eds.) (1972) *Biology Data Book, Vol. I*, 2nd. Edn., Fed. Am. Socs. Exp. Biol., Bethesda, 229–235.

Clarke, J. M. and Maynard Smith, J. (1955) "The genetics and cytology of *Drosophila subobscura*. XI. Hybrid vigour and longevity", *J. Genet.*, **53**, 172–180.

Cohen, B. H. (1964) "Family patterns of mortality and life span", *Q. Rev. Biol.*, **39**, 130–181.

Danielli, J. F. and Muggleton, A. (1959) "Some alternative states of amoeba, with special reference to life-span", *Gerontologia*, **3**, 76–90.

Gerking, S. D. (1957) "Evidence of aging in natural populations of fishes", *Gerontologia*, **1**, 287–305.

Kallmann, F. J. and Jarvik, L. F. (1959) "Individual differences in constitution and genetic background", in *Handbook of Aging and the Individual* (ed. Birren, J. E.) University of Chicago Press, Chicago and London, 216–263.

Lansing, A. I. (1947) "A transmissible, cumulative, and reversible factor in aging", *J. Gerontol.*, **2**, 228–239.

Sacher, G. A. (1959) "Relation of lifespan to brain weight and body weight in mammals", in *Ciba Foundation Colloquia on Ageing. V. The Lifespan of Animals* (eds. Wolstenholme, G. E. W. and O'Connor, M.) Churchill, London, 115–133.

Sacher, G. A. and Staffeldt, E. F. (1974) "Relation of gestation time to brain weight for placental mammals: implications for the theory of vertebrate growth", *Am. Nat.*, **108**, 593–615.

Siegel, R. W. (1967) "Genetics of ageing and the life cycle in ciliates", *Symp. Soc. Exp. Biol.*, **21**, 127–148.

Storer, J. B. (1967) "Relation of lifespan to brain weight, body weight, and metabolic rate among inbred mouse strains", *Exp. Gerontol.*, **2**, 173–182.

Chapter 5

Alexander, P. (1966) "Is there a relationship between aging, the shortening of life-span by radiation and the induction of somatic mutations?", in *Perspectives in Experimental Gerontology* (ed. Shock, N. W.) Ch. C. Thomas, Illinois, 266–279

Anderson, R. E. (1973) "Longevity in radiated human populations, with particular reference to the atomic bomb survivors", *Am. J. Med.*, **55**, 643–656.

Barrows, C. H. and Roeder, L. M. (1963) "Effects of reduced dietary intake on the activities of various enzymes in the livers and kidneys of growing maie rats", *J. Gerontol.*, **18**, 135–139.

Bellamy, D. (1968) "Long-term action of prednisolone phosphate on a strain of short-lived mice", *Exp. Gerontol.*, **3**, 327–333.

Clarke, J. M. and Maynard Smith, J. (1961) "Two phases of ageing in *Drosophila subobscura*", *J. Exp. Biol.*, **38**, 679–684.

Everitt, A. V. (1973) "The hypothalamic-pituitary control of ageing and age-related pathology", *Exp. Gerontol.*, **8**, 265–277.

Forbes, W. F. (1975) "The effect of prednisolone phosphate on the life-span of DBA/2J mice", *Exp. Gerontol.*, **10**, 27–29.

Lamb, M. J. (1965) "The effects of X-irradiation on the longevity of triploid and diploid female *Drosophila melanogaster*", *Exp. Gerontol.*, **1**, 181–187.

Lamb, M. J. and Maynard Smith, J. (1964) "Radiation and ageing in insects", *Exp. Gerontol.*, **1**, 11–20.

Lindop, P. J. and Rotblat, J. (1961) "Long-term effects of a single whole-body exposure of mice to ionizing radiations", *Proc. R. Soc. Lond., Ser. B*, **154**, 332–368.

Lints, F. A. and Lints, C. V. (1971) "Influence of preimaginal environment on fecundity and ageing in *Drosophila melanogaster* hybrids. III. Developmental speed and life-span", *Exp. Gerontol.*, **6**, 427–445.

Liu, R. K. and Walford, R. L. (1975) "Mid-life temperature-transfer effects on life-span of annual fish", *J. Gerontol.*, **30**, 129–131.

McCay, C. M. (1952) "Chemical aspects of ageing and the effect of diet upon ageing", in *Cowdry's Problems of Ageing, Biological and Medical Aspects*, 3rd. Edn. (Ed. Lansing, A. I.) Williams and Wilkins, Baltimore, 139–202.

Miller, D. S. and Payne, P. R. (1968) "Longevity and protein intake", *Exp. Gerontol.*, **3**, 231–234.

Simms, H. S. and Berg, B. N. (1962) "Longevity in relation to lesion onset", *Geriatrics*, **17**, 235–242.

Trout, W. E. and Kaplan, W. D. (1970) "A relation between longevity, metabolic rate, and activity in shaker mutants of *Drosophila melanogaster*", *Exp. Gerontol.*, **5**, 83–92.

Chapter 6

Adelman, R. C. (1972) "Age-dependent control of enzyme adaptation", *Adv. Gerontol. Res.*, **4**, 1–23.

Bjorksten, J. (1974) "Crosslinkage and the aging process", in *Theoretical Aspects of Aging* (ed. Rockstein, M.) Academic Press, New York, 43–59.

Bucher, N. L. R. (1963) "Regeneration of mammalian liver", *Int. Rev. Cytol.*, **15**, 245–300.

Bullough, W. S. (1967) *The Evolution of Differentiation*, Academic Press, London and New York.

Bullough, W. S. (1973) "Ageing of mammals", *Z. Alternsforsch.*, **27**, 247–253.

Coggle, J. E. and Proukakis, C. (1970) "The effect of age on the bone marrow cellularity of the mouse", *Gerontologia*, **16**, 25–29.

Corsellis, J. A. N. (1975) "Neuronal loss in the ageing brain", *Abstr. 10th. Int. Congr. Gerontol.*, **1**, 109–113.

Daniel, C. W. (1972) "Aging of cells during serial propagation *in vivo*", *Adv. Gerontol. Res.*, **4**, 167–199.

Franks, L. M. (1974) "Ageing in differentiated cells", *Gerontologia*, **20**, 51–62.

Grant, W. C. and LeGrande, M. C. (1964) "The influence of age on erythropoiesis in the rat", *J. Gerontol.*, **19**, 505–509.

Harrison, D. E. (1975) "Normal function of transplanted marrow cell lines from aged mice", *J. Gerontol.*, **30**, 279–285.

Hirokawa, K. (1975) "Thymus and Aging", *Abstr. 10th. Int. Congr. Gerontol.*, **1**, 79–80.

Johnson, H. A. and Erner, S. (1972) "Neuron survival in the aging mouse", *Exp. Gerontol.*, **7**, 111–117.

Kay, M. M. B. (1975) "Mechanism of removal of senescent cells by human macrophages *in situ*", *Proc. Natl. Acad. Sci. U.S.A.*, **72**, 3521–3525.

Lesher, S. and Sacher, G. A. (1968) "Effects of age on cell proliferation in mouse duodenal crypts", *Exp. Gerontol.*, **3**, 211–217.

Makinodan, T., Perkins, E. H. and Chen, M. G. (1971) "Immunologic activity of the aged", *Adv. Gerontol. Res.*, **3**, 171–198.

Makinodan, T. and Adler, W. H. (1975) "Effects of aging on the differentiation and proliferation potentials of cells of the immune system", *Fed. Proc.*, **34**, 153–158.

Silini, G. and Andreozzi, U. (1974) "Haematological changes in the ageing mouse", *Exp. Gerontol.*, **9**, 99–108.

Toth, S. E. (1968) "Review article: the origin of lipofuscin age pigments", *Exp. Gerontol.*, **3**, 19–30.

Walford, R. L. (1969) *The Immunologic Theory of Aging*, Munksgaard, Copenhagen.

Williamson, A. R. and Askonas, B. A. (1972) "Senescence of an antibody-forming cell clone", *Nature*, **238**, 337–339.

Chapter 7

Cristofalo, V. J. (1972) "Animal cell cultures as a model system for the study of aging", *Adv. Gerontol. Res.*, **4**, 45–79.

Dykhuizen, D. (1974) "Evolution of cell senescence, atherosclerosis and benign tumours", *Nature*, **251**, 616–618.

Franks, L. M. (1970) "Cellular aspects of ageing", *Exp. Gerontol.*, **5**, 281–289.

Hay, R. J. (1967) "Cell and tissue culture in aging research", *Adv. Gerontol. Res.*, **2**, 121–158.

Hay, R. J. (1970) "Cell strain senescence in vitro: cell culture anomaly or an expression of a fundamental inability of normal cells to survive and proliferate", in *Aging in Cell and Tissue Culture* (Ed. Holečková, E. and Cristofalo, V. J.) Plenum Press, New York, 7–24.

Hayflick, L. (1965) "The limited *in vitro* lifetime of human diploid cell strains", *Exp. Cell Res.*, **37**, 614–636.

Hayflick, L. (1966) "Cell culture and the aging phenomenon", in *Topics in the Biology of Aging* (Ed. Krohn, P. L.) Interscience, New York, 83–100.

Hayflick, L. (1975) "Current theories of biological aging", *Fed Proc.*, **34**, 9–13.

Holliday, R. (1975) "Growth and death of diploid and transformed human fibroblasts", *Fed. Proc.*, **34**, 51–55.

Kay, H. E. M. (1965) "How many cell generations?", *Lancet*, **2**, 418–419.

Martin, G. M., Sprague, C. A. and Epstein, C. J. (1970) "Replicative life-span of cultivated human cells; effect of donor's age, tissue and genotype", *Lab. Invest.*, **23**, 86–92.

Michl, J., Soukupová, M. and Holečková, E. (1968) "Ageing of cells in cell and tissue culture", *Exp. Gerontol.*, **3**, 129–134.

Puck, T. T., Waldren, C. A. and Tjio, J. H. (1966) "Some data bearing on the long term growth of mammalian cells *in vitro*", in *Topics in the Biology of Aging* (Ed. Krohn, P. L.) Interscience, New York, 101–117.

Soukupová, M., Holečková, E. and Hněvkovský, P. (1970) "Changes in the latent period of explanted tissues during ontogenesis", in *Aging in Cell and Tissue Culture* (Ed. Holečková, E. and Cristofalo, V. J.) Plenum Press New York, 41–56.

Chapter 8

Andron, L. A. and Strehler, B. L. (1973) "Recent evidence on tRNA and tRNA acylase-mediated cellular control mechanisms: a review", *Mech. Aging and Devel.*, **2**, 97–116.

Cutler, R. G. (1974) "Redundancy of information content in the genome of mammalian species as a protective mechanism determining aging rate", *Mech. Aging and Devel.*, **2**, 381–408.

Epstein, J., Williams, J. R. and Little, J. B. (1973) "Deficient DNA repair in human progeroid cells". *Proc. Natl. Acad. Sci. U.S.A.*, **70**, 977–981.

Goldberg, A. L. and Dice, J. F. (1974) "Intracellular protein degradation in mammalian and bacterial cells", *Ann. Rev. Biochem.*, **43**, 835–869.

Gordon, P. (1974) "Free radicals and the aging process", in *Theoretical Aspects of Aging* (ed. M. Rockstein) Academic Press, New York, 61–81.

Hahn, H. P. von (1970) "The regulation of protein synthesis in the ageing cell", *Exp. Gerontol.*, **5**, 323–334.

Hart, R. W. and Setlow, R. B. (1974) "Correlation between deoxyribonucleic acid excision-repair and life-span in a number of mammalian species", *Proc. Natl. Acad. Sci. U.S.A.*, **71**, 2169–2173.

Holland, J. J., Kohne, D. and Doyle, M. V. (1973) "Analysis of virus replication in ageing human fibroblast cultures", *Nature*, **245**, 316–319.

Holliday, R., Porterfield, J. S. and Gibbs, D. D. (1974) "Premature ageing and occurrence of altered enzyme in Werner's syndrome fibroblasts", *Nature*, **248**, 762–763.

Holliday, R. and Tarrant, G. M. (1972) "Altered enzymes in ageing human fibroblasts", *Nature*, **238**, 26–30.

Johnson, R., Chrisp, C. and Strehler, B. (1972) "Selective loss of ribosomal RNA genes during the aging of post-mitotic tissues", *Mech. Aging and Devel.*, **1**, 183–198.

Lewis, C. M. and Holliday, R. (1970) "Mistranslation and ageing in *Neurospora*", *Nature*, **228**, 877–880.

Medvedev, Z. A. (1967) "Molecular aspects of ageing", *Symp. Soc. Exp. Biol.*, **21**, 1–28.

Medvedev, Z. A. (1972) "Repetition of molecular-genetic information as a possible factor in evolutionary changes in life span", *Exp. Gerontol.*, **7**, 227–238.

Orgel, L. E. (1963) "The maintenance of the accuracy of protein synthesis and its relevance to ageing", *Proc. Natl. Acad. Sci. U.S.A.*, **49**, 517–521.

Orgel, L. E. (1973) "Ageing of clones of mammalian cells", *Nature*, **243**, 441–445.

Packer, L. and Smith, J. R. (1974) "Extension of the lifespan of cultured normal diploid cells by vitamin E", *Proc. Natl. Acad. Sci. U.S.A.*, **71**, 4763–4767.

Price, G. B., Modak, S. P. and Makinodan, T. (1971) "Age-associated changes in the DNA of mouse tissue", *Science*, **171**, 917–920.

Ryan, J. M., Duda, G. and Cristofalo, V. J. (1974) "Error accumulation and aging in human diploid cells", *J. Gerontol.* **29**, 616–621.

Sheldrake, A. R. (1974) "The ageing, growth and death of cells", *Nature*, **250**, 381–385.

Strehler, B. L. (1967) "The nature of cellular age changes", *Symp. Soc. Exp. Biol.*, **21**, 149–177.

Wheeler, K. T. and Lett, J. T. (1974) "On the possibility that DNA repair is related to age in non-dividing cells", *Proc. Natl. Acad. Sci. U.S.A.*, **71**, 1862–1865.

Wright, W. E. and Hayflick, L. (1975) "Contributions of cytoplasmic factors to in vitro cellular senescence", *Fed. Proc.*, **34**, 76–79.

Chapter 9

Cutler, R. G. (1972) "Transcription of reiterated DNA sequence classes throughout the life-span of the mouse", *Adv. Gerontol. Res.*, **4**, 220–321.

Strehler, B. L. (1975) "Implications of aging research for society", *Fed. Proc.*, **34**, 5–8.

AUTHOR INDEX

178

SUBJECT INDEX